VILLAGE LIFE IN EGYPT.

VILLAGE LIFE IN EGYPT

WITH

SKETCHES OF THE SAÏD.

BY

BAYLE ST. JOHN,

AUTHOR OF

"Two Years' Residence in a Levantine Family,"
"Adventures in the Libyan Desert," "Views in the Oasis of Siwah," &c.

IN TWO VOLUMES.

VOL. II.

LONDON:
CHAPMAN AND HALL, 193 PICCADILLY.

MDCCCLII.

LONDON:
GEORGE BARCLAY, CASTLE ST. LEICESTER SQ.

CONTENTS OF VOL. II.

CHAPTER I.

CHAPTER II.

CHAPTER III.

CHAPTER IV.

CHAPTER V.

CHAPTER VI.

CHAPTER VII.

CHAPTER VIII.

CHAPTER IX.

CHAPTER X.

CHAPTER XI.

CHAPTER XII.

CHAPTER XIII.

CHAPTER XIV.

CHAPTER XV.

CHAPTER XVI.

CHAPTER XVII.

CHAPTER XVIII.

VILLAGE LIFE IN EGYPT,

&c. &c.

CHAPTER I.

Leave Thebes—Beating for Hares—Mountains of Coal—The Ababde—Ombos—Island of Ghanakh—Arrive at Essouan—Picturesque Scene—Old Cemetery—The Seven and Seventy—Syenite Granite—Environs of Essouan—the Town and People—Elephantine—Common Burying-place—View of the River—Secluded Village of Mahatta—Berberi Children—The Cataracts from the Shore—Splendid Scene—Korore—Cunning Hyænas.

FROM Thebes, still proceeding southward, the rocky desert hugging the river more closely on either hand, we came, in due course, to Esneh and Edfou. At both these places our stay was short; but opposite the latter we spent a pleasant morning in beating for hares, of which we got several. There is an immense space of ground here, almost entirely uncultivated, and partly overgrown by dense thickets, partly by a rank crop of halfé. The mountains in the neighbourhood are now called the Mountains of Coal, because that mineral was said to have been found in them by some Frenchman in the Pasha's service. I believe, however, that no such discovery has, in reality, been made; and that in this, as in other similar cases, the will must be taken for the deed. An Ababde village is seen in the distance, on the borders of the desert. Some say that here are the head-quarters of the tribe, whilst others place them at Redesieh. The principal Sheikh has lately bought a house at Luxor, from a Coptic lady, the mistress of a French traveller.

A little after dark, a good wind had taken us among the shoals that precede Haggar Silsilis; and we moored near the Bedawin establishment of El-Hammam. After a cursory glance at the quarries and temples next morning, we went at a spanking rate through the defile; and the breeze still increasing, passed, with a regular sea on, beneath a precipitous range of hills on the west, and halted, out of respect for our plates and dishes, just below Ombos for dinner. Then away again for the frontiers of Ethiopia—the breeze falling off gradually, until the waters became quite calm. The towering propylon of Ombos soon disappeared in the rear, and a succession of lovely reaches, and slips of sylvan scenery in their usual framework of rock, lured us on to where the island of Ghanakh, with its swardy shores and long palm-groves, starts, like a vision, out of the river. The bright lights of sunset were beating, as it were in waves and foam, on the western horizon. It was a scene of exquisite beauty, and I shall long remember it. We stopped at Akabah.

The rocks on either side of the river now begin to assume more varied forms, and to break up into wilder-looking ravines. We proceeded from Akabah with a light wind, and at length reached the term of our voyage at Essouan. The approach to this town is picturesque. The island of Elephantine, green with groves and meadows, and numerous huge bowlders covered with hieroglyphical tablets, break up the river into narrow channels. On the west, huge sandy hills, becoming precipitous here and there, are crowned with ruined convents. On the east there is a fertile plain, terminating in a jagged range of rocks. But the modern city itself is not visible, being concealed by palm-gardens; whilst, towering above it, the ruins of old Arab Essouan form a very marked feature in the landscape.

We passed between two of the bowlders, round which the water dances in giddy eddies, and found ourselves in a lake-like reach, embraced by the island of Elephantine and the east bank. Soon afterwards we had chosen a berth near half-a-dozen other European dahabiahs, and considered ourselves settled for some time. The shore was covered with boats—under repair or in construction—with sheds, and with merchandise just brought down the Cataracts. A little below our station stood an old ruin of classical times, jutting out like a mole, but having served evidently as a bath. On some of the stones were hieroglyphics, but these seem to have been fragments of another building.

Our first walk was to the old cemetery, that stretches far out into the desert, from the summit of a hill descending precipitously to the river, opposite the wall of the Nilometer. The way lies through a small grove, and then through an expanse of ruined brick houses, covering the slope of the hill, and mixed here and there with rocks bearing hieroglyphics and figures in relief. On reaching the summit we had a curious view over the valley of tombs, with its thousands of grave-stones inscribed with Cufic characters, its shattered domes, and huge masses of black rock. On the crest of the hill were two mosques, one old and desecrated, the other spick and span new, neatly whitewashed, and surrounded with a halo of sunshine and sanctity. As far as I could make out—(it is called "The Seven and Seventy")—this building is dedicated to the seventy-seven thousand saints supposed to be buried in the cemetery; and was spoken of in a tone of awe and respect. We, of course, did not approach it; but a woman, who professed to be its guardian, guided us over the old mosque, and pointed out some hieroglyphical tablets on the huge granite bowlders that show themselves here and there.

This cemetery, with the ruined town attached, is perhaps one of the most interesting sights in Upper Egypt to behold, although there is little or nothing to describe. Its extent is great, above a mile either way; and the road to the Cataracts and to Philæ runs through the lower portion, at the bottom of the valley. The whole expanse is dotted with tombs, some consisting of square chambers with cupolas; others vaulted, and of elegant forms: but between these more ambitious monuments are thousands of graves, with headstones about eighteen inches long by a foot broad, and covered with writing. Here and there huge lava-like rocks, crumbling with age, rise up, and give a still wilder appearance to the scene. By day, numerous large black crows, said to be good eating, hop about; but I saw no vultures or hawks. At night, wolves, jackals, hyænas, and phantoms prowl to and fro, and the Egyptian passes in silent haste or speaks under his voice, or, going to the other extreme, sings loudly, to keep his courage up.

At some distance to the east of the cemetery, out in the desert, is the famous quarry of Syenite granite, about which I shall say nothing, except that I have been there; for the little that is to be said has been said a thousand times. The rocks which sweep round the plain of Essouan are black and dismal-looking, broken up into ravines and gulleys, where, although the footsteps of hares are frequently seen, I did not notice the slightest trace of vegetation. Here and there are scratched a variety of hieroglyphical characters. In the flats below, the silk-tree rises in regular rows, as if planted by the hand of man; and the colocynth plant winds its snake-like forms over the sand. The fruit was just beginning to ripen. All about, the tracks of hares, as well as of wild beasts, are visible, showing the courses they take in going down at night to the seyals, or water-ponds, where the irrigation-wheels are placed, to drink. With the exception of some scattered plantations to the east, near the Quarter of the Blacksmiths, almost the only fertile land near Essouan consists of a few gardens to the north, surrounded with mud walls, but containing little except palm-trees. They are intersected by dusty lanes, and all the foliage in them is grey with dust. But on the river-bank there is a nice strip of sward, shaded by some acacias, where we used to go and smoke our pipes towards evening, and watch, over a broad expanse of sand, the shining semicircle of the Nile, almost ever dotted by sails. This was below Elephantine; so our view was uninterrupted to the Libyan shore, which rose in rocky swells or sandy slopes. A large ruined monastery stood on a bold spur exactly opposite.

The town of Essouan itself is extensive, but thinly inhabited. There is a shabby sookh, very ill provided with merchandise. Many of the houses, however, are large and respectable looking. The population are different in aspect from ordinary Egyptians; long, thin faces, tolerably fair, and aquiline noses, abound. On the way from the centre of business to the mooring-ground, near the old bath, there is a steep path round a huge mass of bowlders, from the clefts of which some trees spring, and cast a pleasant shade. The sides of the rocks are covered with hieroglyphics, as, indeed, are most of the rocks and stones in this neighbourhood, both on the banks and in the river. It is read, or guessed, that the inscriptions record the visits of kings and other distinguished personages to this interesting region, which may well be called the Gates of Egypt.

The island of Elephantine cleaves the waters of the Nile immediately opposite Essouan. At its northern extremity it is low, even, and covered with groves and fields, intersected by little walks bordered by reed-fences; but to the south, there is a great swell of rocks and rubbish, with a few inform ruins. As we wandered among these we came to an oblong building, some two or three feet high, with several openings at one side. This, we were told, was the common burying-place of the island. The corpses of the dead Elephantinites, dressed in their ordinary clothes, are shot through one of the openings, and sent to decay with their forefathers. It is not, of course, to be supposed that there is anything irreverent meant in this way of disposing of the departed. Circumstances, institutions, superstitions, vary the form of burial among various nations, but the natural feelings remain unchanged. The Greeks burned their dead, certain tribes exposed them to be devoured by wild beasts; we make manure of them; the ancient Egyptians pickled them; but I have no doubt that the practisers of all such customs think other customs unnatural and barbarous, and wonder at the depravity of their neighbours. The people of Elephantine are of the Berberi race, black and well-featured. Some of the girls had delightfully expressive countenances. They wear, under the ordinary fellâh blue robe, what may be called a short petticoat, composed of an infinite number of leathern thongs. Several of these interesting articles were offered for sale, and there would appear to be a great demand for them among travellers.

A wide view of the river, broken up by rocks and islands, some barren, others fringed with vegetation — between almost precipitous banks—is obtained from the southern point of Elephantine. The Cataracts do not, properly speaking, extend so far; but the waters still seem hurried and agitated, and ripple and foam against every obstruction. We remained long gazing at this wild scene, where not a sign of life, except an occasional boat stealing along— not a single habitation, except a ruined convent in the depths of a great valley on the western shore, withdrew our thoughts from dealing with the pure forms of nature.

In one of our rides about the neighbourhood of Essouan we fell upon a quiet place that interested us exceedingly. Proceeding through the valley of tombs some distance on the way to Philæ, we turned off across the range of dismal-looking rocks that extends in apparently unbroken grandeur to the right, and, entering a rugged defile, made for the river. We expected to find some granite-bound shore mirroring itself in the pure waters, but, to our surprise, fell upon a little Berberi village, called Mahatta, built in a sheltered nook. The path suddenly became a road between diminutive gardens, protected by neat mud walls, and then a street with nice cottages on either hand, shaded by one or two pensile palms. A few women, who were streaming along in the scorching sunshine, paused to look at us, and pressed the little ones they were leading closer to their sides; but we passed on unaddressed until we came to the rocky beach, that sunk sheer to the river. Here we sat down to rest and meditate on the singular scene. A little fragment of the Nile, between an island and the main, surrounded on all sides by black, stony mountains, which it reflected, stretched at our feet, tranquil as a mountain lake. The few trees of the village that waved their tufts of leaves overhead, and here and there, at wide intervals, a dwarf sant springing from some cleft in the rocks, alone contrasted with the mighty desolation that reigned on all sides. Yet there was nothing gloomy in the prospect. A sea of light glowed everywhere, from the depths of the sky to the depths of the water, and seemed to gather like a halo round the far-up peaks of the swarthy hills.

A number of little children of Satanic hue,

but with fine ingenuous features, came to offer carved sticks ornamented with wire, and spears cased with the skin of the warran, or great water-lizard, for sale. They bargained boldly, and showed great unwillingness to part with their goods unless for a fair price. Only the elder ones could speak Arabic, and they but badly. All were much interested by the ticking of a watch, and wondered what kind of animal it was.

Our boat was not too large to enable us to ascend the Cataracts, but we did not make the attempt; and were reduced, therefore, to view that wonderful scene from the shore. The path turns off from the road to Philæ, a little above the village of Mahatta. We were soon amidst the shattered piles of rock that form the characteristic feature of the whole neighbourhood. It was near sunset when we arrived. We had, indeed, but just time to cast our glance over the scene before the red orb of the sun neared the horizon with its lower rim, and lengthened out into the shape of a balloon of fire. On all sides—on the western and the eastern bank, to the north and south—rose a mighty amphitheatre of ebon rocks, hurled into heaps like lava round the crater of a volcano. The river was dotted with a thousand stony islands, round which the prodigious current, as it rolled down its sloping bed, hissed and roared, and eddied, and foamed, and sparkled. The reflexions of dying day, thrown in, like a fiery liquid into a giant witch's caldron, mingled with the sombre tide for a while: but soon it flowed opaque and grim; and as the imperceptible sounds of day were hushed, an ever-increasing roar, a tumult of struggling waves, louder and louder as light faded and shadows gathered, came rushing to our ears.

We remained for some time listening to this mighty crescendo of the cataract, and then descended to make our first cursory examination of the details in the few moments of light left to us. A black boy, who had offered himself as guide on his way to his village, pointed out the various Babs or Gates, and seemed to take pride in the terrible to-do which Nature made in that spot. Neither measurements however exact, nor words however charged with meaning, can convey a proper idea of the impressions beneath which the mind thrills at the aspect of this scene. We wandered on in religious silence, passed unheeding by a little American boat moored in a quiet cove above the great gate, and arrived, when night had quite thickened over the landscape, at the secluded village of Korore. Here our guide left us without asking for a reward, and we turned off into the desert to make our way back by a smoother road. As we went, our donkey-drivers entertained us with stories of wild beasts and ghouls, and sang with strained energy as we approached the great cemetery and saw its thousand white tombstones shining palely in the moonlight. Among other things, they said that hyænas are blessed with more than human cunning, and have a knack of kicking dust and sand into the eyes of those whom they have marked for destruction, in order to blind and render them an easy prey.

CHAPTER II.

Visit to Philæ — Start — Cross the Cemetery — Berberi Village — Nubian Black-mail — Civil Beggars — The Nile above the Cataracts — Afloat — Difficult Navigation — First View of the Temples — Cursory Examination of the Island — Morning View from a Propylon — Sound of the Cataracts — Official Boundary of Egypt — Ruined Mosque — Scene from its Summit — Great Heat — The Old Man's Dike — Legend of a Black Robber.

The plan of our journey did not include a visit to Nubia, where a totally different people from that we had hitherto beheld would have presented itself, living by the side of monuments of a similar character. We were content, therefore, to proceed to the island of Philæ, which, although surrounded with a Berberi population, is within the limits of official Egypt. It lies a mile or so above the commencement of the Cataracts, as Elephantine lies below; and as the lower island seems to check the course of the waters, and restore to them their even, complacent flow, so the upper island, thrown with its companion Biggeh into the middle of the stream, seems, by huddling the divided current into narrow channels, walled with rock and encumbered by the ruins of mountains, already to begin hurrying and goading it as it were for the thousand leaps it is about to take.

We delayed our visit some days, in order to become intimately acquainted with the neighbourhood of Essouan; but at length, having formed a party, started on a fine cheerful morning from the boats, mounted on a pack of excellent but somewhat ill-favoured donkeys. Having passed beneath the screen of trees that bounds the view some fifty yards from the river, on the top of the sloping bank, we pushed gaily along the lane bordered by ruined houses that leads to the cemetery. Broken walls, desolate chambers, fragments of arched cellars, laid bare by treasure-seekers, surrounded us on every side as we trotted up the slope, the prospect widening as we ascended. Then we got among the tombs, that lie principally over a broad valley stretching north and south between shattered heaps of rock—a granite avenue, most imposing to behold. Strings of camels or droves of donkeys, bearing merchandise, occasionally passed us. A man offered for sale a pretty golden locket and chain, of European manufacture, which he had found, but asked too high a price.

The road is level and easy for some distance through the desert beyond the cemetery; but when the defile leading to Mahatta and the pathway over the rocks to Korore were passed, we got among a series of rugged defiles, that reminded us somewhat of our Libyan donkey-ride. These passed, we soon came to a straggling village of neat houses, shaded by great sycamore-trees, the largest I have seen in Egypt. It was a quiet, pretty scene. The women, many of delicately-formed features, came to us, holding little sable brats in their arms, and with a sweet smile asked for *backsheesh*—a kind of black-mail under a pleasant form, which we were not so churlish as to refuse. Children that could walk ran along by our sides, holding out their hands and crying "*Inshallah terooh be selameh!*" "If it please God, may you go in peace!" One small chap, being at first disappointed, repeated the cry at least twenty times; and when we pushed a-head unheeding, as a trial of his temper, dropped behind, but, instead of pursuing us with curses, as many a disappointed sturdy beggar or trained boy-mendicant, does in Europe, kept faintly murmuring the kindly wish—“*Inshallah terooh be selameh!*”

Issuing from the village and the trees, we came to a broad open space, frowned over by a pile of Cyclopean rocks. At the further extremity was a busy crowd and a number of masts, announcing the presence of a ferry-station. Men were shouting with innocent fury; and women, bless their hearts! with every appearance of real ferocity; donkeys, sharing in the general excitement, brayed gloriously; and camels, as they knelt down to receive their loads, complained of the kicks on the shins they received in pig-like grunts. We paused a moment whilst our man looked out for a boat, and gazed at the broad Nile, which burst as it were in sheets of light from the rocky ravines to our left, and, after spreading and eddying in a perfect plain of water, disappeared amidst low stony islands on our right. Near us were some palms and sycamores; but the opposite shore, and all the rest of the framework of the glittering current, rose in barren swells or rocky angles to meet the pure blue sky.

Our course lay between the island of Biggeh and the eastern shore—up a narrow channel, through which the current, meeting every now and then with ledges of outlying rocks, or great rounded bowlders, rolls with impetuous force. The light puff of wind that dropped at first into our sail carried us diagonally from the starting-point into a little creek indenting the island, where it left us whirling about, in danger of being dashed against the stony banks or the concealed rocks that everywhere abound. Ropes and poles were soon brought into play, however; and a man with a couple of active lads, scrambling over black rugged points or creeping along narrow ledges, tugged us slowly against the stream. On either side rose huge heaps of rocks covered with bowlders, that seemed to threaten every moment to roll down and crush us. Some were piled one on the other like rude pillars, and reminded us of the ruins of Druidical temples. Here and there a few shrubs, with twinkling green leaves, waved from high-placed crevices, as if to show that the principle of life lies concealed everywhere, even where death and desolation endeavour to exert undivided sway. Presently the rocks appeared to sink—to recede on either hand; and the towering ruins of Philæ sprang into sight, sparkling like a palace of snow amidst congealed billows of lava. Our first impression was a feeling of incongruity. The gem was too lively for its sombre setting. Vast pillars quarried out of the living rock—mountainous propylæa, squatting amidst heaps of rubbish, and covered with the stains and scars and wrinkles of age—horrid colossi, dumb but stern-looking—cavernous colonnades, such as distend the eye and compress the lips in more tranquil districts, as they rise and expand at the extremity of telescopic vistas of foliage, would here have been in keeping; but not that white and elegant pile, which appears, as the wilderness of granite is cloven by the shining stream as by a silver sword, to totter in the sunshine far above a belt of verdant and waving groves. By degrees, however, we became reconciled to the contrast, and beheld in that group of pale temples an emblem of the one hope that goes before us, beckoning amidst the dreary desert of life, beautiful at a distance, but, if ever reached, found to be a mere mockery, a ruin, a receptacle of dust, rubbish, dry bones.

We struggled some time with rope and pole in sight of the island, still keeping beneath the frowning precipices of Biggeh; but at length came to a point where a breath of wind favoured, when we glided along the bend of the river eastward, beneath some lofty pillar-like bowlders engraved with hieroglyphics, to the steep bank of Philæ. We were soon engaged in a first cursory inspection of the vast cluster of ruins, of which the plan was already in our heads. Here we saw the temple, with its great lofty walls; there, diminutive chapels, that looked happy in ruin amidst the embraces of bright green trees; further on, spacious courts surrounded with colonnades; there long porticoes, with a perfect labyrinth of shrines and chambers; passages leading to the summits of towering propylæa, or to little terraces, or down to the water's edge; altars, obelisks, heaps of shattered masonry. No detailed description can convey a proper idea of this singular island, which seems of old to have bristled throughout its entire extent with holy structures, and to have been surrounded with a massive wall of solid masonry. Time and other agencies have been at work to degrade the beautiful scene, but have only succeeded in producing another kind of beauty. Vegetation seems to have aimed at filling up the lacunes of architecture. Trees and shrubs wave over all the northern part of the island, and grasses have sprung up everywhere.

We passed the night in one of the chambers, or rather landing-places, on the roof of the temple; and next morning went up to the roof of one of the propylæa to see the sun rise. Looking eastward, we seemed to be standing in the centre of a number of concentric circles. First came the ruins, and then a thin screen of trees, and then the river, and then a strip of vegetation; beyond that a segment of desert bounded by a great curve of hills. All around the same series appeared, to a greater or less extent; but beyond the river, to the westward, rose at once the abrupt forms of Biggeh. When we reached the summit and stood on the roof, the sky was already beaming with light, whilst the valley lay wrapt in gloom. The river, grey and calm, that clasped the island like a belt, was here and there dotted by a pale sail, scarcely filled with the cold breath of dawn. Dew lay still on the eyelids of Nature, though they seemed to thrill already at the touch of the first faint threads of light. A dream-like silence brooded around, except that far away could be heard, through the rocky gateway—opened, like those that lead to the children's Babylon, "as high as the sky," for the passage of the Nile—the solemn roar of the river as it tumbled into the land of Egypt. We were listening intently, when a golden beam struck the propylon, and presently temple, tower, and grove, and river, seemed to awake from their slumbers, shake off the last traces of night-poetry, and compose themselves a sober demeanour for prosy day. No buzz of stirring life came to the ear —where was it to come from?—but, nevertheless, the roar of the Cataracts seemed to recede like the murmur of a retreating army, and at length utterly died away.

During our stay in Philæ we left no corner unvisited, and studied as hard as if we intended to come out in the learned and topographical line; but I have promised to abstain from such discussions. Suffice it to say, that during our two visits we passed our time most pleasantly, and learned rapidly to look upon it almost as a home. Among the excursions we made during our stay, was one to an old ruined mosque situated on a spur of the Arabian chain, some distance south of Philæ. It marks the official as well as the traditional boundary between Nubia and Egypt, although the Berberi population, or at least the portion known as Shellalees, or Cataract-men, has pressed lower down. A little ferry-boat took us to the shore, on a steep bank of lupines, where we had given a rendezvous to our donkeys. A narrow path led thence to a little village, surrounded with reaped dhourra fields. The houses were tolerably neat, and over the door of one of them we noticed an English dinner-plate, with the Chinese bridge-and-pagoda pattern, built in as an ornament. The people all hereabouts seemed, as far as we could judge, a quiet and simple race. A few blacks, probably slaves, and women, were working in the fields.

The path now led along the river through groves and villages, on a narrow strip of land beneath the mountains and the Nile, rarely more than a hundred yards wide. The houses were sometimes built against the rock in a line, with two or three rows of sycamores in front, a bank covered with lupines, and then the river. Dismounting at the foot of the slope on which the ruined mosque is situated, we soon reached its threshhold. Little remains except the tottering and long since desecrated minaret, up which we climbed with some misgivings. The winding staircase is in many places broken, and may one of these days prove treacherous beneath the foot of some incautious traveller—for none but travellers now visit this mosque, the sacred reputation of which has been transferred to an apparently spick-and-span new building a little further on. We were rewarded for our pains by a glance over the broad, unbroken stream of the Nile, the whole mighty volume of water on which the land of Egypt depends for its existence. To the south, our view was soon shut in by rocks; but to the north we could see the three ravines which the river pierces trident-wise, between the islands of Biggeh, Philæ, and the main, on its way to the Cataracts.

I have said little about the heat experienced during this journey, because, being tolerably well seasoned, we seldom noticed it. The state of temperature that mostly attracted our attention was the bitter cold of some of the mornings. On this day, however, we found the sun about noon somewhat oppressive, and were not sorry to reach once more the roof of the temple of Philæ, where, during the remainder of the day, we smoked our pipes in a patch of eternal shade, cast by a propylon, and talked, not of the Alps or Apennines, but as the place suggested, of Ptolemies and Pharaohs, and various other interesting gentlemen of the olden time.

In returning from Philæ we followed, in some parts, a new road. Crossing to the main, we at once struck into a desert and made for a defile, through the promontory of rocks that advances here towards the river. We were soon removed from the sight of all vegetation, but not from traces of past civilisation. A wall of crude bricks, in some places double, at places tolerably lofty, but often reduced to the condition of a long mound, skirts the road. Most probably it is the continuation of the same wall, which at various points, principally at the entrance of ravines, is to be traced nearly the whole length of the valley of the Nile; but I will not venture to assert to what mythological emperor it owed its construction. The Arabs call it the Old Man's Dike—Gisr el Agoos; and believe themselves to possess authentic traditions of its construction. They and the learned agree on one point, that it was erected for the purposes of defence—like the Chinese wall, and others nearer home. These vain attempts to fortify whole countries seem to have been common in ancient times, especially towards the decline of empires.

A ruined watch-tower, perched on the summit of a solitary rock, was pointed out as the scene of a terrible story. A gigantic black—all blacks in Arab narratives are giants—is said to have made it his repair, and to have levied during a long space of time forced contributions, accompanied often by murder, on all passengers whose numbers did not overawe him. At length the Government, jealous at this interference with their prerogative, sent out a party of soldiers to put a stop to it. The black made a desperate defence, as robbers and other wild beasts will when brought to bay, and refusing to surrender was killed; or rather, in his despair, feeling that all was over, leaped down the rock, and dashed himself to pieces on the road.

CHAPTER III.

People of Essouan — Welees — Tradition adapted to Circumstances — An unlucky Practical Preacher — Peculiar Race of People — Ancient Egyptian Language — Origin of our Crew — Characters of the Men — Goomma, our Jack-of-all-Work — Reis Suleiman — Nile Etiquette — Charm against the Evil Eye — The Steersman; his peculiar knowledge — Mustering of the Crew — Rationale of the Down-voyage — Storms on the Nile — Start — Akabah and Koubanieh — Koom Ombos — View of the Ruins by Night — Lights on the Plain — The Silk-tree — its Medicinal Value — Amazons of Gebel Molair.

THE people of Essouan, as I have said, are different in appearance both from the peasantry of the neighbourhood and from ordinary fellâhs. They claim to be descended from a colony of soldiers, planted there "in ancient times and seasons past;" and are somewhat remarkable for bigotry and superstition. The tombs of their deserted cemetery they regard not as those of mere ordinary mortals, but as belonging to Welees and holy men of all kinds, buried, as a lad told us, some hundred thousand years ago,—indeed, before the time of Mohammed Ali! Many of them say that all the saints of Egypt have a commemorative headstone here. However this may be, it seems certain that the innumerable tablets, covered with Cufic characters, that meet the eye in every direction, are invested with supernatural power; and every now and then an old tradition is revived in a new form, to the effect that a dare-devil Turk, a drunken Arnaout, or an infidel Frank, has been punished for firing at them by instant death, or at least by the fracture of a limb. It seems certain that some foolish traveller, not many seasons ago, took a shot at one of these holy monuments, that his gun burst, and that his arm was broken. After such a confirmation of their belief, it would be rather difficult to persuade the Essouanees to renounce it; and as respect for the dead and the places where they lie is one of the greatest guarantees of civilisation, I see nothing to be gained by the success of any sceptical preacher on the subject. The individual, therefore, who suffered, accidentally or otherwise, in endeavouring to show the Arabs the absurdity of their belief, must not consider himself as martyr in a good cause, and may be well content that he was not subsequently mobbed and cudgelled. What would be the fate of a foreign gentleman, who should take it into his head to walk into the churchyard of some English country-town, and commence making a target of the records of the inimitable piety or unexampled goodness of rustic or squire?

In the neighbourhoood of Essouan, and for some distance below, is a curious race of people, very distinct from the ordinary fellâhs, and equally distinct from the Berberis, although confounded with them by many travellers. They are very dark, almost black, but speak Arabic, and claim to be pure Egyptians. The most obvious way of accounting for their origin, is to say that they are produced by a mixture of the two contiguous races; but this does not appear to be the case, and I should rather be prone to believe that there is Negro blood in their veins. Their hair has a strong tendency to crisp, their lips are full, their nose flattish, with very conspicuous nostrils. I do not give this, however, as an absolute portrait of the race; for the type is very fluctuating, and many individuals have nearly Egyptian features under a black mask. All speak, as I have said, Arabic; but some in a tone so squeaking, that it requires attention to discover, when they jabber among themselves, that they are not using some Soudan dialect.

I greatly object to founding a theory on one or two isolated facts; but may not the Berberi language contain some traces of ancient Egyptian? *Ombo*, in that language, is the name of a date-tree, and *betté* of the fruit. The latter word reminds one of the word *batés*, given by Diodorus Siculus as meaning "fruit."

Most of our crew came from the neighbourhood of Essouan, which, indeed, furnishes a very large contingent of men to the Nile fleet. The country seems to abound with all the conditions favourable to population, except one—namely, space. The mountains come so close down to the shore, that only a narrow strip of land is left, with a little nook here and there, a kind of green creek of vegetation running in between the black granite cliffs. The principal villages are Koubanieh and Akabah, from the first of which came five or six, and from the second, three of our men. All these people were fine honest fellows, well united by the ties of relationship and local patriotism. I shall always remember the cheerful face of Goomma, or Friday, a slim lad, who during a great part of the journey escaped from the labours of tracking or rowing by being appointed by Sid Ahmed to the office of scullion, under-cook, washerwoman—maid-of-all-work, indeed. It is the custom for one of the crew to be selected for this office. I expected that the comparatively easy life led thus during several months, would disgust Master Friday with the hard work to which sailors are often called; but I overheard him once talking to Sid Ahmed, and steadily rejecting the idea of becoming a traveller's servant, and thus making his fortune. All his ambition was, he said, to become a reis, captain of a good boat, and to spend his days in that honourable employment. The position he coveted is attainable by any intelligent and steady mariner in the end, and I hope his desire may be fulfilled.

Reis Suleiman, captain of the "Zeyn-en-Neel," our fast-sailing beauty, was from Lower Egypt, and a quiet, respectable, cautious man. Whilst we were under sail I used often to go and sit in the bows of the boat, and listen with interest and profit to his talk. He was no babbler—not a narrative man, but a man of aphorisms; and when he told a story, it was always to illustrate some moral truth. He had very strict ideas on Nile etiquette, and when our clipper would positively commit the unpoliteness of passing some other traveller's boat under full sail, endeavoured to keep to the other side of the river, lest we might seem to exult over the defeated. He was partly, perhaps, influenced by fear of the evil eye; for when the position of certain sand-banks or the narrownesss of the channel compelled us, unless we chose to take in sail, to dart by one of the ordinary slow-coaches, like a gazelle past a lame camel, some of the crew invariably ran to stick a knife in the mast as a charm of protection.

The mustamil, or steersman, next in rank, was a giant, if I remember rightly, from Akabah. He seemed to know the position of every sand-bank, island, palm-grove, and village in the country— was, in fact, a walking index to the map of Egypt. In another department of knowledge he was equally proficient, and professed to know the names and qualifications of every dancing-girl in Egypt, from Kutchuk Hanem (Madam Kutchuk) of Esneh; or Hosneh-et-Tawalee (Hosneh the Tall), and Bomba-el-Gobtaniyeh of Thebes; down to Zibeydeh of Dishné, or Ayshe of Reramoon. The wags of the crew said that the tender epithet of Baba was bestowed upon him in every along-shore village, from Atfeh even unto Essouan.

Of Samson, or Abu Noor, I have already spoken. We had left him at Ombos to spend some time with his relations; others had been dropped at Akabah and Koubanieh, in going up; and all belonging to the neighbourhood had obtained leave to go and kiss the babes born since their last visit: for most of them were married. Those from the nearest spot received orders to muster on a certain day; and making their appearance in due time, enabled us to start on our return journey exactly on the day determined.

It is the custom, when once a boat has reached the term of its voyage, to take down the mainmast and all the yards, and trust, in descending, to the current and the oars. North winds are indeed so prevalent in the spring, that sails are rarely of any use; and what would be gained by them occasionally would be lost on other days by the resistance offered by the bare poles to the wind. Some idea of the violence of the storms that frequently blow may be formed from the fact, that even with masts and yards displaced, and with the assistance of a current of nearly four miles an hour, it was impossible for our fourteen steady oarsmen to make any way. I have seen a rope broken in an attempt to track down. The most violent gales begin to blow near noon, increasing in strength for some hours, but generally falling away towards sunset. The men work very cheerfully until late at night, provided they are not forced to waste their energies uselessly against the resistless north wind.

We started, then, with an incomplete crew, from Essouan one morning, and passing one of the narrow channels, through the line of breakers stretching from the point of Elephantine to the shore, made for Koom Ombos. Our progress at first was slow, for half-a-dozen oars were scarcely sufficient to man our galley. When we reached the open river, we met two boats belonging to European merchants, or pedlers on a large scale, on their way to Kartoun. At Akabah and Koubanieh we stopped to take in the rest of our crew. Most of them came down with their families, bearing huge baskets of dates and bundles of mats, for sale in Alexandria — a profitable venture, considering there was no freight to pay. One man, a little behind the rest by accident, shot out from a point on a triangular reed raft, which supported him and his luggage as he swam to the rudder. At length we were fully manned, with the exception of the invaluable Samson, and were soon dashing by the green groves of Ghanakh.

Evening found us still plying the oar along calm reaches towards Koom Ombos, where we arrived some hours after sunset. It was a bright moonlight, and we determined to take a first cursory view of the ruins. So we climbed the steep bank, jumped the water-courses leading from the shadoofs, and soon reached the foot of the enormous tower or pylon, which terminates the southern horn of the semicircular fortification of the ancient city. The principal ruin stands in the centre, half buried in sand, which has swept over the ruined brick walls, and formed a kind of glacis within and without. The plan was not very evident by night; but the effect was wonderful of those huge squat columns supporting a roof, each stone of which was many tons in weight, and which cast a shadow seemingly of corresponding heaviness. On ascending the highest point of the wall, we had a wide view over the desert and the plain on either side of the river. Lights were sparkling here and there, probably in the tents of Bedawins, or near some of those temporary huts of palm-branches constructed by the fellâhs when on night duty.

Next day, after a more attentive view of the ancient Egyptian ruins and remains of Saracenic houses, we strolled into an expanse of halfé and bushes beyond in search of hares; but though a Bedawin lad and his dog came with us, we did not get a shot. The silk-tree is plentiful about here: some of the fruit, or rather pod, was still green, looking like an unripe apple; in other cases, a beautiful rosy blush overspread the side embraced by the sun. At a more advanced stage of ripeness the pod opens, and masses of silken floss burst forth from about the curved cone of closely-set seeds. The juice is used as a poison in various ways, especially in order to blind children, to save them from the conscription. They say it is mixed with milk, and drank medicinally by women. On the edge of the halfé ground are some bushes, beyond which the desert rises in an easy slope. A few huge vultures sat here and there, seemingly in a meditative mood.

On leaving Ombos we saw some crocodiles upon banks of sand, but in this, as in other cases, shot at them in vain. Near Gebel Molair we expected to find a hare-ground, but were disappointed. We heard a tradition of some Amazonian race of women in these parts; but it was so confusedly told, that I did not quite understand it. The upshot, however, was, that the women, dissatisfied with the way in which affairs were conducted by the male sex, had taken the government into their own hands; and like the possessors of authority in other countries, had decreed the sweets of idleness to themselves, and the duty of labour to their subjects.

CHAPTER IV.

Defile of Haggar Silsilis — Arab Traditions — Evening Scene—Man-created Abysses—Plain of Silwa—Rocky Desert—Wild Beasts — Sporting Bedawins —The Valley of Inscriptions — Small Tombs discovered — Excavations — Curious Mummies — Cost of Mummification — Our Bedawin Guides — their Mode of Life — Arms and Ammunition — News of unexplored Tombs and Ruins — Colocynths and Sakarân — Resolve to return to Farés — Excursion — Companions — Traces of a Temple — Humble Cemetery — Act as Resurrectionists — Extraordinary Sarcophagi — Ancient Portrait-carvers — Bowls for the thirsty Dead — Ruined City of El-Birqeh — Information from Report — Hidden Treasures — Return to the Plain of Silwa — Ramadeh — Plain covered with Bowlders — Canal — Inscribed Rocks.

THE defile of Haggar Silsilis is one of the most remarkable points in Upper Egypt. The Nile from Essouan has flowed through the centre of a vast basin, the widest point of which is about Ombos. Here and there the mountains advance towards it in detached masses, whilst in many parts the desert slopes gradually away. But at Silsilis two mighty ridges from the east and west draw near the river. The western ridge reaches it, and throws down its precipices into the stream; but on the east, a broad valley, level in many places, but covered with hillocks in others, separates the main body of the mountains from what may be called an advanced post—a huge mass of sandstone, an island of rock forming one side of the defile. As you approach from the south, the first opening in the ridge that appears is the dry valley, which I once thought to have been the ancient bed of the Nile; but soon the isolated mountain on the right hand, and the Libyan promontory on the left, seem to open for the passage of the stream.

On both sides as we shot down — the oars scarcely taking hold of the rapid current — we saw immense traces of quarrying: vast caves, subterranean temples, streets hewn through the living rock. Near the bank was a meagre fringe of vegetation, here a line of silk-trees, there the pendant branches of the safsaf, a kind of dwarf willow, with various shrubs peculiar to the country; but aloft was nothing but stone, tossed or carved into all imaginable shapes. The Arabs have an idea that the excavations on both banks are the remains of a city of peculiar construction, and in their legends tell marvellous things of its history. Here dwelt the prince who, in old times, stretched a chain across from shore to shore,—to enable him, some say, to levy contributions on passing boats; say others, to stop the progress of an invading fleet. Twilight was thickening as we glided past, and out of the dimming forms on either hand enabled us easily to figure to ourselves fragments of giant palaces and superhuman fortifications. We moored at the northern entrance, under a kind of willow-hedge, near a small tuft of palms on the east bank.

I shall never forget that hot morning's ramble through those mighty sandstone quarries, those deep-cloven rocky avenues, those vast abysses, not formed by some convulsion of Nature but by man with hammer, chisel, and lever. Ever afterwards the wonder in viewing the Pharaonic monuments was, not that they were so large, but that they were so small; for we knew that Silsilis had, after all, made but a feeble contribution to their materials, principally derived from mountains disembowelled on either side of the Nile throughout its whole course.

We were moored at the extremity of the plain of Silwa, which stretches north and east, and is tolerably fertile. The village was situated at some distance inland. On the other side the rocks still continue to keep close to the river, leaving a mere thread of land, principally covered with black bowlders, between them and the sloping bank. We crossed, dropping down to a place opposite Silwa, and moored for the night. I climbed to the summit of the ridge of rocks, and beheld the desert sweeping away in black billows to the horizon. All the surface of the rocks was like lava, but underneath the stone seemed fine-grained and good. Here and there in the gulleys, amongst which I descended, were places where the crevices had been scraped for a kind of yellow earth used as soap. I did not see a bird or a sprig of vegetation; but in the ravines leading to and from the river, the sand, sifted down by the wind, was maculated with the footsteps of the hyænas, wolves, and jackals, that had gone down the night before to drink. In all these parts it is common to see little semicircular inclosures of loose stones built on ledges of rocks.

Here the settled Bedawins, still inveterate sportsmen, lie in wait on moonlight nights, to watch for the wild beasts as they slink along to assuage their thirst.

Next morning we ascended a few hundred yards, in order to be opposite a place discovered in going up, and called by us the Valley of Inscriptions. It was a deep cut in the ridge, running in for a great distance, with here and there figures of the size of life, engraved on the smooth precipices, and a great number of small inscriptions, containing a variety of cartouches, pronounced to be of very old kings. After proceeding some distance, there was a sudden rise in the valley and an immense sand-drift. We turned to the south, across the hills, and came to a lofty point overlooking the river. Here was a cluster of excavated tombs, some of which had been rifled long ago, but apparently not by antiquarians. Others were still closed with large stones and dirt, and curiosity induced me to have the entrance of one of them cleared out, in spite of certain keen compunctions about violating these humble last resting-places. On the very summit of the hill appeared to have been a kind of square building, probably supporting a cupola, like those which now cover sheikhs' tombs. Fragments of wrought masonry were scattered round, and a square foundation for the wall cut in the rock, about a foot high, still remained intact. Within this little enclosure we set to work. At first we found only a long trench, in the shape of a coffin cut out, but empty; but in a corner, having cleared sand and rubbish to the depth of four or five feet, came to a rough stone, still apparently in the position in which it had been placed when the tomb had been last used. Having removed this we crept into a little cave, in which there was scarcely room to stand up, but the flooring of which we found to be composed of many layers of mummies imbedded in sand. Most probably the cave had at one time been quite full, the space left appearing to be produced by the settling down of the bodies during many thousand years. On examination, the mummies were found to have been laid on a kind of back-board, formed of palm-sticks placed close together, to which they were firmly swathed. There were no paintings of any kind on the cloths, and everything seemed to indicate that we had broken into a tomb reserved for the very humble orders. I have seen a ridiculous calculation somewhere — ridiculous, because based on no sound data whatever — that the cost of mummying a corpse was, in ancient Egypt, from *four to two hundred and fifty pounds sterling.* May I be allowed to estimate the cost of producing these mummies as having been under three-and-sixpence?

We carefully replaced the grim fellâh whose remains we had disturbed in his tomb; and, somewhat ashamed of having acted as resurrectionists, sat down to talk with our two guides, of whom it is now necessary to say a word. They were young men, Bedawins, from the little village of El-Hammâm, which we could see on the slope of the hill to the south, not far from the entrance of the defile of Silsilis. One was named Abd-el-Mahjid, like the Sultan of Constantinople, although in the third word the accent is thrown back to the penultimate; the other, Ismaeen. Fine honest lads they seemed to be, good specimens of their race. They said they belonged to the tribe of Ababde, which have occupied both sides of the river to the exclusion of the fellâhs. Their mode of life, although their section of the tribe has long been settled, still smacks strongly of the desert. They cultivate the little ground they possess, producing principally dhourra and barley; but they likewise bring up camels and donkeys for sale in more populous districts. At certain seasons of the year the young men set out with droves of these animals for the lower country, and our two friends had pushed as far as Keneh, Girgeh, and Siout.

It is probable that very little intermixture with the Egyptian race has taken place in this out-of-the-way colony. Most of the people we saw were of genuine Bedawin physiognomy. Abd-el-Mahjid had married the sister of Ismaeen; and the two seemed united in the bonds of close friendship. They were always anxious to be together, and had, it seemed, performed all their journeys in company. Keen sportsmen both, and admirable shots, each possessed a gun; and during our stay we had but to express a wish for jugged hare, and a copious supply of the raw material was almost at once brought. They showed us also little traps, in the shape of cross-bows, used to catch wild pigeons, which they scarcely consider worth powder and shot. Ammunition is rare and expensive, and the smallest quantity as a present is thankfully received. Most of the inhabitants of these parts possess arms of some kind; light javelins, with long, thin, triangular heads; swords, straight and with large crossed hilts; daggers worn strapped to the arm, above the elbow, often in company with an instrument for extracting thorns, of constant use to people who generally go barefoot. Most of these weapons are very plain, and of inferior materials. The guns, valued at from one to three pounds by Ismaeen, are sometimes curiously ornamented with a coating of wire; the stock is often entirely covered with the skin of the warran; as are the javelins and the ends of their huge clubs.

These young men told us that at a little distance to the south of Haggar Silsilis, — on the west bank, likewise, — at a place called Rasras, were other tombs and the remains of a temple. Furthermore, that at a day's journey inland existed the remains of a whole city. Our curiosity was excited, and we closely questioned them. They kept steadily to their statement, and professed to have examined both places; and we at once began to discuss the propriety of getting up one of our sails, and returning to explore this new ground.

After some further wandering in the neighbourhood, we returned towards our boat. On ledges of the rock heaps of gathered colocynths were drying in the sun; and at the entrance of the Valley of Inscriptions, in little shallow hollows, a kind of alluvial deposit, an Egypt in miniature, created by rain-showers that fall in I know not what season, produced thick patches of a plant called sakarân. The seeds of this plant, which resemble sesame-seeds, produce intoxication, as the name imports, and even death. Robbers are said to use it in order to stupify or poison their victims.

It was determined in the afternoon to go back, at least as far as Farés; so we got up the trinket or fore-sail, and by close of evening were again dashing through the defile under a thin veil of clouds, pierced easily by a bright moon. We moored under a steep bank for the night; and next morning found half the population of Farés, men, boys, horses and donkeys, looking down at us. We had soon made our selection of bare-backed beasts; and throwing our great-coats across them to deaden the edge of a very razor-like ridge which most exhibited, galloped away over dhourra-stubble, by tufts of the castor-oil plant, through a thin palm-grove, leaving Farés to the right, and soon came to the edge of the desert. About twenty guides, companions, or friends, accompanied; some on foot, one on a fine horse, and four huge fellows on two little asses. As we proceeded, others left their work in the fields, and ran to join us. Several of the men possessed very hideous physiognomies; and more than one was disfigured by some frightful skin disease. Like most Bedawins, they were impertinently familiar and inquisitive, without the least intention to annoy. Abd-el-Mahjid and Ismaeen, who had relations in Farés, were perfect gentlemen in comparison to the others; and probably did not boast in claiming to be the sons of the most distinguished men. They could both write very neatly, and set down any words I asked them accurately and well.

After passing by Rasras, a little village scattered over the first swells of the desert, we saw a long row of white mounds a-head, with a few palm-trees waving above; and were told, "There is the temple." We had some doubts, at first; but soon found that the account given us had been in the main correct. On rising over the mounds, which possibly mark the line of a brick enclosure, we saw a considerable space, about ninety paces in length by twenty-three in breadth, covered with remains of walls of solid masonry, but in no instance remaining intact to the height of more than two feet. The forms of some chambers, the position of doorways, could be distinctly traced. Many of the stones were covered with hieroglyphics; and it was suggested that the monument dated only from the time of the Antonines. The Arabs assured us that they remembered seeing this temple rising to the height of two men; and said that it had been covered by the sand. Possibly the wind periodically uncovers what yet remains, but many of the stones must have been carried away.

Proceeding some hundred yards to the west into the desert, we came to a large piece of swelling ground, covered, as it appeared at a distance, with white spots. These were small gatherings of sand, and marked the position of tombs, the well-entrances of which had been filled by the wind. Some of the tombs were open, and rifled; and one of our party, just about to enter, was restrained by seeing an ugly-looking snake wriggle away from the mouth.

We determined to be sacrilegious once more, and set the Bedawins to work to scrape out the sand from one of the largest wells. In about an hour they succeeded in uncovering a huge stone that stopped up the entrance of the tomb or cave, excavated in what appeared to be alluvial soil, into which we got in spite of the stifling heat and revolting stench. It was full of mummies, layer on layer; but the only interesting point we noticed was that they had no back-board of palm-sticks. They were simply swathed, and lacked ornaments of any kind. Our guides had promised us painting and gilding, and were annoyed by the disappointment. They began scraping in another place, and came to an immense quantity of earthen pots, all more or less broken and empty. A third trial introduced us to a cave filled with curious sarcophagi, without any traces of hieroglyphics. One was of stone, and quite plain. The others, about the size of a large coffin, were of a coarse kind of red earthenware. The lids, merely laid on, were ornamented with rude faces—the drollest caricatures of humanity it is possible to imagine; huge comical noses, goggle eyes, and grinning mouths. Possibly they were intended as portraits of the departed, all being cast in a different mould; but certainly the artists had disdained flattery. The wise have set down Cleopatra as no beauty, on the evidence of a portrait they pretend to have discovered; but, even if intended as a likeness, it was, most probably, a failure. The Egyptians could not make the portrait of a tree—even their geese are problematical. Why should they have succeeded in petrifying upon their walls the lovely features of the Serpent of Old Nile? I am inclined to think they failed, as certainly the Lawrences of old Rasras failed: for never was the human face divine convulsed into a resemblance with these coffin-lid alto-reliefs. Even the visages of the originals, which we saw beneath —the skull scarce covered by a thin mask of blackened flesh and tight-stretched cloth—were less hideous. It is true that, in a few cases, some error of the artist's hand had introduced a grotesque leer or a supernatural grin; but this strange portrait gallery was only rendered more awful thereby.

Some of the mummy-cloths found here bore traces of painting; and in the stone coffin, probably belonging to a Sheikh-el-Beled of those days, was a fragment with thin streaks of gilding. A good number of bowls of fine earthenware, in perfect preservation, were strewed about; and it struck me that it must have been a superstition among the ancient peasants, that at certain seasons their well-swathed and well-pickled ancestors sat up in their coffins, and, draining draughts of some infernal wine, passed the hours in as much jollity as to mummies is permitted. Looking round the dim cave, which smelt of death and corruption, I imagined the upstarting of these grim wassailers, the jostling of those below, the polite shrinking of those above; and as I could not help conceiving them with physiognomies such as glared from the coffin-lids, called into existence a most horrible picture, which makes me shiver even now.

Our guides had wonderful things to tell us of the inland ruined city, which they called El-Birqeh. They said it was situated in a south-west direction from Rasras—some said, at a distance of a short day's journey; others, from sunrise to sunset; others, six or seven good hours. On the way were traces of an old road. All agreed that the ruins, situated at the foot of a ridge of precipitous rocks, were of great extent. It would take a day to examine them, said one. There were tombs, but no quarries that they knew of. The ground was covered with stones, bearing writings and figures of all kinds. The shortest road is from Bemban, but the best from Farés.

I had previously seen the mountains of Birqeh from the walls of Ombos, and they were subsequently pointed out from the rocks of Silsilis. They form a very bold feature on the horizon, and seem to be an isolated group. If at the distance of a day's journey, they must be very lofty. I greatly regret not having been able to visit them, especially as Ismaeen assured me that in the neighbourhood were concealed inexhaustible treasures, destined to be the property of the person who should find and draw a certain magical sword, also very carefully hidden.

I have never read any notice of the Valley of Inscriptions, of the tombs on the hill near it, with their peculiar mummies, or of the temple or the tombs of Rasras. Possibly (though this is not likely) they have been often visited and been deemed unworthy of mention; but, for my part, I was equally interested by these traces of the ancient country-people as by the tombs of kings and high-priests. No doubt there were several villages or small towns in this district of old, that owed their existence or their prosperity to the neighbourhood of the quarries of Silsilis.

In the evening we pulled down again to our former station at the head of the plain of Silwa, and next day spent several hours rambling among the quarries in search of hares, which were found to be tolerably numerous. A fox was also started. A little before sunset we strolled along a lane that now wound among palm-trees, now amidst dense thickets, now across open fields, to an expanse of bushes near the village of Silwa, where hares were seen every now and then sitting in open places, or starting up under our very feet. Here we remained till moonlight, and then returning, pulled down the stream a little below Hammâm.

Next day we went to Ramadeh, where we landed to explore the neighbourhood. Just above our mooring-ground, near a meagre clump of palms, was the entrance of a broad canal with high banks, now perfectly dry. It was nearly parallel with the river, along the foot of the rocks, and probably in inundation time communicates with the plains of Edfou. Crossing this we came to the entrance of a vast ravine, which entered the hills with a gradual slope, and so smooth a bottom that I thought at first it must have been the work of man. At length, however, it broke up as it were into numerous smaller veins. I climbed to the top of a rock and viewed the stony country beyond with interest. At some distance to the south-west was a small plain, covered, it appeared, with huge black bowlders, that looked like the ruins of a city. All about were small caves, some natural, others apparently dug in search of the yellow earth I have before mentioned.

Turning to the south, along the principal branch of the valley, I rose over the ridge that separates it from the plain of the Nile; and beheld another ravine conducting apparently in the direction of the seeming ruins I had witnessed. At its mouth, or rather in the midst of the plain in front of it, was a cluster of bowlders, that attracted my curiosity. On approaching I found them to be covered with hieroglyphics, containing cartouches; scratched figures of men on horses, armed with spears; large-horned bulls, &c. The idea struck me afterwards that the bowlders I had seen in the interior may be similarly engraved. To the east, half way to the river, was a curious cluster of rocky columns, apparently natural, though some of them may have been artificially arranged. At a distance they looked like the ruins of a Pelasgic temple. A deserted stone fellâh village stood near the entrance of the canal, and had probably been erected by the people employed as navigators.

CHAPTER V.

Edfou — Ruined Village on the Temple — Sporting Excursion — Coptic Convent — Hares — El-Kab — Necropolis — Ancient Paintings — Curious Thorn — Esneh — News from the Upper Country — Settlement at Agono — Free-Trade — Coin in Favour — The Cry of "Backsheesh" — Arabs calumniated — Alms-giving in Christian Countries.

We arrived at Edfou, and visited the temple, one of the most perfect remaining in Egypt, although not properly cleared out. On the roof are the remains of Coptic houses, built of unburnt brick. We made a sporting excursion along the gisr, which zigzags to the foot of the distant hills, over a plain, still in a marshy state near the town, and almost a lake towards the west. Pelicans, storks, cranes, herons, cormorants, geese, ducks, teal, divers, paddy-birds, hawks, kites, crows, vultures, in inconceivable profusion, covered the water and the fields, or dotted the sky;

and as we approached the dry land, a constant procession of flights of partridges, all moving from south to north, passed overhead. We found them sitting in immense numbers among the halfé grass, and on the sand-hills beyond.

Near the end of the gisr was a Coptic convent, or village, which we visited. The court was encumbered by a number of hovels; the church, with four altars or recesses, contained a few rude paintings, but no inscriptions. We had been told by the Arabs that it was built over the entrance of a vast cave; but the priest, a polite old gentleman, denied that this was the case. Around were numerous tombs, some cut in the face of the rock, others with well-entrances; but no sculptures or ornaments of any kind. The halfé plain was covered with flocks of sheep and goats, guarded by dogs of surprising fierceness, black and large, totally different from the curs of Lower Egypt.

In the evening we crossed to the opposite bank, where we had found hares in going up, and beat about amongst the large clumps of bushes. Several long-eared gentry were startled; but our principal amusement consisted in noticing the myriads of drowsy sparrows that flew up, and settled down again, as our men threshed the boughs. Next morning we started for El-Kab. Here we visited the vast earthen fortifications of the ancient city of Eilithyas; now used as manure-mines by the peasantry; and the rocky necropolis to the north. It consists of an isolated mountain, very nearly resembling the Gebel-el-Mouta at Siwah. We ran over the principal tombs. They are small in themselves, but communicate by pits and rugged passages, with very large unsculptured caves, destined no doubt for poor relations and slaves. The sculptures, which are supposed to be of high antiquity, represent scenes of domestic and agricultural life in a very quaint and amusing manner; but in a style inferior to the paintings on Chinese porcelain. A good deal of information has been derived from them on ancient Egyptian manners.

The whole hill, on all sides, is honeycombed with excavations, some of which are reached by neatly cut staircases in the rock. Many niches seemed calculated for receiving the mummies of children, if children were ever mummied. In the valley behind the hill was an isolated rock, with two or three excavated caves, reached by doorways, the lintels and jambs of which were dimly ornamented with hieroglyphics. We returned by a path leading to the north of the great enclosure, and noticed a curious kind of thorn, with contorted branches covered with prickles, and said never to bear leaves, but producing a kind of red berry, some of which still remained, and were of an agreeable taste.

At Esneh, where we visited and admired the portico of the temple, now perfectly cleared out, we met an Essouan acquaintance. He was a Piedmontese, on his way back from Kartoon and the White Nile with several boats full of gum. He had spent about a year in the upper country, and had succeeded in disposing of the merchandise he took with him, and in purchasing his cargoes, in spite of the interference and opposition of the Pasha governor. The account he gave of the regions north of Kartoun was very satisfactory. According to him, the tribes, with the exception of the Shlouks, just beyond the limits of the Egyptian empire, were quite tame and hospitable, and well disposed to trade, if let alone. The furthest country visited in that direction, he said, was Agono, of which the king, or chief, was a man of liberal disposition, anxious to enter into relations with foreign merchants. The priests even had been allowed to form a settlement there, and were only sent away because the Turks, in jealousy, persuaded the ignorant natives that they were sorcerers, who wickedly cast blights on their crops.

Our informant gave us a curious instance of the danger and absurdity of interfering with commerce. A Turk was made governor of some place on the Blue River, and began to trade with the Gallas. The speculation was at first profitable; for his customers were delighted to find a market without going to Abyssinia. But, not satisfied with reasonable gains, the Turk at length acted like a Turk, established a monopoly and put in practice several arbitrary measures. Almost instantly merchandise ceased to arrive, and the trade which he had so well begun was entirely extinguished.

On the White Nile are found mines of excellent iron, but it would not pay as an export. Gold dust is brought down in fair quantities, as also ivory and other valuable articles. Gum abounds. The money preferred is Spanish dollars of the time of Charles IV.; good Egyptian piastres are also liked. A kind of cheap onyx is valued by the women at forty or fifty piastres, and rings of amber are received almost as money. These facts I set down as stated by our Piedmontese friend, because, from his peculiar point of view, he is likely to have observed correctly.

Many travellers complain, very pathetically, that from one end of Egypt to the other they were assailed with one continual cry for "backsheesh." There must be a good deal of exaggeration in this. It reminds me of the Frenchmen who constantly hear us English saying, "Yes, yes, very good," because these are the only words of our language they know. Travellers arrive generally with this one scrap of Arabic already in their possession, and fancy it is used on every possible occasion. As I have already said, it is appropriate in the mouth of every man who has performed a personal service, and observes that you forget to remunerate him in the accustomed way. In some few districts, the women squatting by the roadside, or men working in the fields, having noticed instances of indiscriminate generosity on the part of Franks, try it on, if I may use that expression; but their hope of success is so vague, that should you stop as it were to comply, their first impulse is to run away. Professional beggars, of course, persevere; but the cry generally proceeds from impudent children, who do not pronounce the word in a supplicating tone at all, but as if they had noticed that it exasperates some touchy persons. Thus at Esneh, a dozen brats, black and brown, dogged us as we strolled round the walls, barking out, "*Backsheesh, ya Khawagah! backsheesh, ya Khawagah!*"—as if they thought they were uttering a direful insult. One little fellow, especially, worked himself up into perfect fury—he might have been calling us dogs or Jews from his manner—and when we turned round, made a bolt away in such bustle that he threw his head into the eye of one of his companions, and both rolled upon the ground. After a small turn-to with the injured one, he returned to the charge; but when we held out some few fuddah pieces, he could not be induced to approach near enough to take them. The sweeping calumny to which I allude has its origin, no doubt, in the irritable virtue of the Political Economist school, which will thankfully receive a pension, but consider it a damnable sin to give a penny.

It is reported that one of our modern Collegiate ladies, being persecuted at Benisouef for alms by a multitude fit to wait round the pool of Bethesda, called for a policeman in order to give the whole of them in charge. With some difficulty her dragoman explained to her, that, not being in a Christian country, it was perfectly lawful for these poor people to ask from those who were willing to give; but that, being in a Mohammedan country, he would take the liberty, if she wished it, of falling upon the unhappy wretches whip in hand. The lady having told him not to hit *very* hard, went musing along through the lane which he at once created, and was naturally led to examine the question of the connexion of Church and State. Marvellous is the power of logic! Guided by the unconscious hint of Botchy, and working from the premise firmly established in her mind, that "indiscriminate charity"—a pleonasm for charity itself, in these days when "true liberty" means despotism—is *the* error to be scouted, she soon perceived the absolute incompatibility of the actual regulations of our social system with the whole body of the Christian doctrine—which our legislators, nevertheless, hypocritically invoke as a sanction. Being of undoubted courage, she accepted the consequence unhesitatingly; resolved that no form of belief which inculcated the duty of affording gratuitous relief to our fellow-creatures should be tolerated in a civilised land, threw her Bible overboard, and enrolled herself at once under the banner of what is now called philosophy.

CHAPTER VI.

Carnac — Medamot — Wild Pigeons — Ancient Brick Houses — Dancing-girls — their Quarter — An Arnaout Party — The Bouluks — Egyptian Venus — A Supper after the Manner of the Turks — Vocal Statues — Dog-Latin — The Tourists scolded — Practice of Writing on Ancient Monuments — New Mode of Puffing — The Tombs of the Kings — Ancient Paintings — Conventionalisms — Battle Scenes — Art of the Egyptians — Progress in modern Times — A lofty Mountain — Extended View.

THE following day we pulled down to Thebes, where we a second time visited all the celebrated ruins. Carnac is, in truth, a wonderful place, and it is easier to fall short than to exaggerate in describing it. There are no pillars so gigantic, no gateways of mortal construction so massive, in the world; and the vast series of courts, chambers, colonnades, sanctuaries, contain objects of curiosity so numerous that I doubt whether, after repeated explorations, we noticed more than one half. It is to be regretted that Government has established a gunpowder factory close at hand, and that more than one of the pylons has been used as a limestone quarry.

I rode across the fields to Medamot, where, besides a temple, are the remains of a small town of brick houses. The path, which is circuitous, led through rich plains, with the ruins and groves of Carnac always at the same distance to the left. On the way, huge flights of wild pigeons settled on patches of grass, and though we passed through their midst, scarcely condescended to flutter out of the way of the donkey's feet. They crowded so close together, that six, seven, or even ten, could be brought down with one shot. Although the temple of Medamot will stand comparison with no other on this plain, being small and very imperfectly preserved, the visit interested me, because here only I saw traces of the private life of the ancient Thebans. Probably the ruined houses still existing are not of very great antiquity, but they are built with the large brick used in the enclosures of temples. It is curious that everywhere else, except in the tombs, only public monuments remain. The reason, no doubt, is, that in old times, as now, most private dwellings were built of very flimsy materials, and that the bulk of the population lived in hovels. The houses of Medamot, which were uncovered by the fellâhs digging for manure, have small rooms, but very thick walls.

Our mooring-ground was at Luxor. One evening some of our party went out to see the dancing-girls, who are now more common here than at Esneh. Their quarter consists of a little cluster of hovels outside the village; but although a self-appointed guide professed to know the dwelling of every one of the celebrities, he took us to see nothing but a set of hideous blacks, or coarse-looking fellâhas, with whom dancing was a mere sham. One pretty little girl performed a little better than the rest, but she was evidently of the same category. We returned, therefore, towards the boat, despairing of seeing the celebrated beauty, the Venus of the boatmen, Hosneh-et-Taweelee; but when we passed the head-quarters of the Arnaout garrison, heard sounds of merriment, and learned that the principal Ghawazees had all been pressed that night into the service of the Bouluk.

It was proposed to us, and with some hesitation determined, that we should invite ourselves to join the party. The application was received with politeness, and the master of the house himself came out to introduce us. Presently, therefore, we were comfortably installed in a large room, dimly lighted with oil-lamps, upon divans, with pipe and fingan in hand, in company with as strange a set as it has ever been my lot to associate with. The Bouluk himself was a genteel sort of ruffian enough. He was treating another Bouluk, just arrived from Esneh—a great, burly, drunken, roaring villain, who was rolling about in the place of honour at the upper end of the room. About half-a-dozen other Arnaouts, all of cut-throat physiognomy; a few handsome, quiet men, said to be Circassian Memlooks; the Sheikh-el-Beled, and other magnates of the village, sat around; and near the door was a crowd of inferior people, Arnaouts and others.

There were seven or eight dancing-girls, all more or less agreeable. The principal one, Hosneh herself, was really a tall, elegantly-shaped, beautiful woman, and would have attracted admiration and applause in any European ballroom. Her eyes, which, as is the custom, she generally kept half-closed in dancing, the lashes sometimes even resting on the cheeks, seemed, when they opened and beamed around the room, to fill it with redoubled light; her nose, her mouth, her chin—every feature—was exquisitely moulded; and nothing could exceed the beauty of her arms and hands. In this instance, fame had fallen short of the truth.

I will not describe the performance of this Egyptian Aphrodite—as superior to Kutchuk as a pine-apple to a potato—because I should have in a great measure to repeat what has been said in another place. Hosneh, however, but slightly overpassed the bounds of delicacy, and gave real pleasure by the supple elegance of her movements. Both herself and her companions seemed under the mark in animal spirits, and went through their task with very little enthusiasm, refusing even to drink the arraki that was offered. It is probable, therefore, that what we were told was true; namely, that their services were forced and gratuitous. It is the custom to make presents at the end of every applauded dance, or, at any rate, towards the close of the evening; but not a para made its appearance. We asked the Sheikh-el-Beled, in a whisper, whether we should give the girls something; but he said by no means, as the Arnaouts would be offended.

If we were in a generous mood, however, we might make a present to the servants at the door!

When the ladies had retired we wished to retire also, but we were told that there was a supper toward, and our benevolent-looking hosts insisted with uproarious hospitality that we should stay. Napkins were brought and spread on our knees; then came round a metal ewer and basin. We washed our hands, and were soon dipping our fingers into a series of genuine Turkish dishes. Most of them were of excellent flavour, and highly creditable to the taste of the cook. Afterwards we smoked a pipe, listened awhile to the spluttering ruffian from Esneh, as he roared out insulting jokes upon the decent Circassians, calling them slaves bought with gold, and boasting of being a Scodri; and then escaped, half stifled with a supper, which had been literally almost forced down our throats, and with the close atmosphere of the room, to our boats. A couple of bottles of wine, sent back by the servant who lighted us home with a lantern, amply paid for the hospitality which we had to a certain extent extorted.

The western plain of the Theban valley, with

its overhanging mountains, presents far more numerous objects of curiosity than the eastern. We here revelled in temples and tombs from morning to evening. The Vocal Statue was, of course, visited; and a witty companion wrote on the basement—"*Mem: non. audii.*" The same wag used to prove that Egypt was not created by the Nile, from the philosophical axiom, "*Ex Nilo nil fit!*" I may add, that this was the only occasion on which any of our party wrote upon rock or monument. For my part, I have always made a point of abstaining from inscribing my name. In some cases the practice may be harmless enough; and it is interesting to find the signature of a celebrated person—Bruce, for example—in an out-of-the-way place. But why every vulgar tourist, in these modern days of steam navigation and tranquillity, when travelling in Egypt is easier than travelling in Wales, should think it necessary to commemorate his presence—not once, modestly, in an unoccupied corner, but fifty or a hundred times, and, by preference, in the midst of an inscription, or on the cheek of a painted or sculptured goddess—I cannot understand. The Columns of Carnac, the Tombs of the Kings, the Pyramids, the Caves of Beni Hassan—every monument, in fact, from Philæ to Alexandria—are defaced by the names of obscure individuals of all nations, either carved minutely or daubed in black letters of colossal size. A clever Maltese, understanding the value of puffing, has taken care to announce in various places that he is the best dragoman in the world. The Arabs, following up the elegant example, not only write their names and sentences from the Koran, but sketch caricature resemblances of steamers, animals, and even men. From this the passage is easy to wanton destruction; and when we add the combined efforts of antiquaries and Turks, it is really surprising that anything remains in Egypt worth visiting. I do not despair, however, of seeing every inscription rendered illegible, every painting effaced, every statue pulverised, every temple reduced to a heap of chips and rubbish.

A month might be spent among the tombs alone, without any sense of weariness. Their variety is infinite, and, like all great works, they seem grander on a second inspection, and grander still on a third. The Assasseef sepulchres are the most extensive; but the Biban-el-

Melook are incomparable. A rocky pass, precipitous on both sides, takes you round behind the hills of Gournou, towards a mountain with a pyramidal summit, which, though not made with hands, serves as a majestic mausoleum. In its lower spurs the tombs—some thirty long galleries, expanding here and there into chambers, are pierced. I shall never forget the impression produced as we wandered slowly down their inclined floors between the richly-painted walls, beneath the strangely-ornamented roofs. Egyptian art seems here to have reached its highest state of perfection, several degrees below the point at which Italian art had arrived in the age of Cimabue. The principal thing to be admired is the beauty of the colouring in a mechanical point of view; for not the slightest artistic feeling is displayed. The colours are laid on flat and even, and remain in admirable preservation. The Raphaels of ancient Egypt beat our painters and decorators hollow, but as draughtsmen were wofully deficient. Some eyes, accustomed to dwell upon their caricatures, actually admire the beauty of the forms, the expression of the countenances, the graces of the composition; and in one or two groups discover traces of perspective! I could see nothing of all this. The forms appeared to me ill-drawn, and only faintly resembling nature, like school-boy sketches on a slate. The faces have one uniform stupid stare; the drapery is about as flowing as a deal board; composition there is none. The figures are generally arranged in long lines, and their occupations are expressed in a merely conventional manner. I have read animated descriptions of battle and hunting scenes beheld in these and other places. A battle is represented by a king six or eight feet high, with his legs stretched out like compasses, shooting with a bow into a compartment containing a profusion of Lilliputians. A sportsman, in like manner, is a giant taking aim at a little square frame, just at the point of his arrow, containing stags, wild boars, wild fowl, &c., huddled higgledy-piggledy together. I am inclined to think, that the very small progress in the arts made by the ancient Egyptians is a proof that their empire was not of so long duration as is supposed.

It was not, therefore, as works of art that I admired and wondered at the representations on the walls of the Tombs of the Kings; but as ornaments exhibiting a taste verging sometimes towards grossness, a great fertility of fancy, and much mechanical skill in the execution. As sculptors, the Egyptians seem to have made more progress than as painters. It is true, their statues are all stiff as corpses; but there is sometimes great finish and beauty about the features. As to the idea that the genius of artists was restrained within certain limits by laws or customs, I believe it to be a mere fancy, invented by the strange partiality of travellers and archæologists for the objects of their studies. It is more probable that artists were restrained by their own want of talent and knowledge. No doubt, as we are told, tradition required certain symbols, certain forms of costume to accompany each god or goddess; but the same was the case in Greece, where the Thunderer, the Huntress, the Messenger, and every other mythological being, had, as it were, their uniforms; and modern art adheres with almost absurd rigidity to certain recognised modes of draping and adorning its St. Jeromes, its St. Johns, its Virgins, and Our Saviour, yet never complains that its genius has too little space to move in.

There is an evident progress in Egyptian monuments of post-Pharaonic times; although, singularly enough, some antiquaries look with contempt on these recent productions, and reserve their praise for beauty of design, boldness of execution, exquisite finish, and so forth, for the uncouth attempts of the most barbarous antiquity. The only figures of real sublimity, irrespective of size, I have seen in Egypt, are those of the women supposed to represent the heavens, that embrace some of the astronomical subjects in the small chambers on the roof of the temple of Dendera. They remind one of Blake's wonderful designs, but, because they are the work of mere moderns, obtain not the suffrages of amateurs.

We determined, on our second visit to the Gates of the Kings, to ascend to the summit of the pointed mountain that overhangs them. It was a breathless piece of work; and when we came to the path that leads down along the edge of giddy precipices to the valley of the Nile, almost felt that we had done enough. However, after a moment's pause, up we went again, and at length, on reaching the summit of the peak, were rewarded by a most magnificent prospect. Not only was visible the whole plain of Thebes divided by the winding river into two semicircular expanses of green, sharply contrasting with the yellow desert, that stretched on either side to the foot of the rocks, but to the south the Gebelein, or Two Mountains, half way to Esneh, seemed almost at our feet; and to the north the eye could travel as far as the great reach of Negadeh, and even to the ridge of hills sweeping in from Keneh on the way to Kosseir. Immediately beneath us were the numerous defiles or glens formed by the projecting base of the hill, and filled with ruins and tombs of all dimensions. To the right was Gournou; then the Memnonium; the two statues on the plain; Medinet Habou; beyond were Luxor, Carnac, and Medamot—all distinctly visible as on a map. Behind, the desert-hills rolled away; and along the side of one a white streak was pointed out as the direct road to Farshoot.

CHAPTER VII.

Conscription in Upper Egypt—Regular Method of raising an Army—Modern Improvements—Meddling Foreigners—Alarm created in the Country—The People fly to the Hills—Places of Refuge—Scene from the Great Peak—a False Alarm—an Underground Palace—Dance of Grief—Embarcation of Recruits—Melancholy Spectacle—Procession of Mourners—We are unjustly Cursed—Keneh, the deserted Town—Exploit of some English Travellers—Signification of Arms in Egypt—Dangerous Mania—Call on an English Agent—Singular Effect.

During the winter of 1850-51, his Highness Abbas Pasha thought proper, say some, to supply the deficiencies created in his army by death and various causes—say others, to increase the total number of the troops, in prevision of a struggle with the Porte. Whatever the motive, it is certain that an order for a conscription went forth; and by the time we returned to Thebes from the Cataracts, had been partially executed, and was known throughout the length and breadth of the land.

In the good old times of Mohammed Ali, a levy of troops much resembled a slave-hunt. Men were seized without any warning, wherever they could be found; and the operation was performed so rapidly that, although an immense amount of misery was created, it was accompanied by comparatively little disturbance. The conscripts were cast, bound hand and foot, into the boats, and thus transported to head-quarters, where, by a liberal application of the koorbash, they were soon converted into slipshod heroes. Their wives generally followed them on foot, and such as did not perish by the way contributed to increase the pauper population of Cairo and Alexandria.

As is well known, the Egyptian mothers prefer maiming their children to allowing them to be taken away for military service. Thus, some extract their teeth, whilst others put out one of their eyes, either by means of sharp needles or the milky juice of the silk-tree. I have seen a lad whose foot had been held over a fire when he was young, in order to lame him, that he might be preserved to his parents.

Young men also maim themselves, when their mothers have omitted the tender care, either by some of the above-mentioned means or by cutting off one or two of their fingers. Mohammed Ali's one-eyed regiment has often been mentioned.

It seems to have occurred to the advisers of Abbas Pasha that the method pursued by his grandfather was highly barbarous and uncivilised. He resolved, therefore, to proceed on an entirely new plan—to organise a conscription in regular French style, and to take so many men from each district according to its population. At first sight, if we admit the necessity of an army, this seems a reasonable mode of proceeding enough; but in practice it caused more protracted suffering, and introduced more disturbance into the country, than the brutal proceedings of the great Pasha.

I have often heard persons, in whose minds the immoral idea that one man may rightly be governed and disposed of by another is ineradicably fixed, whilst deploring as in duty bound individual cases of misery, speak with admiration of any vigorous proceeding by which "big, idle fellows," as they are pleased to call the Egyptian peasantry, are made to work, whether as soldiers or otherwise. But the truth is that the fellâhs, as I often take occasion to repeat, are not more idle than other men; and besides, if they were so, the proper means are not taken to reform them. They object, very properly, to being industrious or patriotic, "on compulsion." Hold out inducements suited to their character and capacity, and they will be ready to become soldiers, or navigators, or whatever you please. Pay them well, and with regularity above all; do not allow them to starve under their uniform, and complain, as I have heard them, that even their belts, however tightened, cannot repress the pangs of hunger; enable them to live without begging or knitting stockings, or trafficking ignobly on the beauty of their wives. This would be the way to destroy the prejudice against military life, and to prevent Egypt from becoming a region of maimed, toothless blinkers. As to any other method, more or less civilised, of robbing people of their right to dispose of their own time or labour in their own way, small is the credit of whomsoever may advise or introduce it. Indeed, if violence is to be the order of the day, the rapid summary practice of

Mohammed Ali was far preferable to the hypocritical device adopted under his grandson.

On the present occasion, the duty of carrying out the conscription, instead of devolving on the Nizam, or regular troops, was entrusted entirely to the Sheikhs of the villages, with power to call in the assistance, when necessary, of that estimable rural police, the Arnaout cavalry. Perhaps these officials were never engaged in an operation at once so invidious and so profitable. The Sheikh of Luxor, for example, had to provide twelve "active young men"—such was the tenor of his order—but he was given *carte blanche* in the selection. What an opportunity for indulging any private hate, for straining a point in favour of a friend, or of a father who was willing to purchase indemnity for his son! The fortunes of the whole country population (Cairo and Alexandria found favour and exemption) were placed for a time at the mercy of a class of men, already so well disposed to be tyrants.

No sooner did news of the intentions of Government circulate, than the whole country was thrown into a state of perturbation. Almost all work was suspended. Boys, young men, every one who supposed himself liable to seizure, fled away to the mountains, or hid in the places of refuge prepared for such an emergency by the people of old times. Every valley, every glen, every cave, quarry, and tomb, considered to be out of reach—not those, for example, visited ordinarily by travellers—were at once filled with fugitives. Wherever we went thenceforward, our movements were watched by files of men, squatting on the spurs of the hills, or moving in parallel lines with us along the giddy summits of precipices, which we could not venture to climb. Of course it was impossible for all these poor wretches to provide themselves either with sufficient food or with water. Their friends brought them the former, but they generally had to come down at night, along with the hyænas or the wolves, to drink at the pools or canals nearest their retreats. Sometimes, even, they remained a great part of their time in the villages, protected by their numbers, until the Sheikh summoned the assistance of the Arnaouts. At the first notice of the approach of these hated ruffians, for whom lookers-out were set, there was a general rush towards the hills. When I was on the top of the great peak before mentioned, that overlooks the plain of Thebes, a false alarm was raised at Gournou; and presently numerous long lines of men appeared hastening up the slopes, and plunging into the ravines—all bound for the tombs. When they reached their place of safety—from which they could always retreat farther into the desert, if necessary—they began rolling large stones down the slopes, to show that they were ready to defend themselves; and throughout the day occasionally we heard the crashing sound of these projectiles, as they jumped from crag to crag towards the plain. I believe in no instance did the recruiters venture a pursuit, being content to keep watch at the foot of the hills, and to catch any one whom starvation or weariness induced to descend.

When we went down into one of the private tombs with our guide, who from age and other causes was exempt, he amused us by speculating on the time for which a man could hold out in such a retreat. The passage, almost as steep as a well, was narrow and winding, and in descending we had to work our way, feet downwards, laboriously, and in some danger of suffocation from heat and dust. I do not know what the actual depth was; but the time we took in working down, down, like moles, made it seem as if we had penetrated several hundred feet below the surface of the earth. At length we reached a beautiful chamber, supported by four elegant pillars. The walls were painted in brilliant colours on a white ground, and seemed as fresh as when the eye of the artist had alone admired his work. The ceiling, purposely made to undulate, for the sake of effect, was covered with a magnificent vine-tree, fruit-laden; so that we seemed to be in a subterranean garden. Our guide, though hackneyed in burrowing, re-echoed our exclamations of delight; but it soon appeared that he regarded the tomb merely as a place of refuge. In his opinion, a man might live any length of time there—a week, a month, two months, as long as his provisions or his patience lasted. I objected the stifling atmosphere; but he said that heat was healthy, and seemed to have floating in his mind the wild stories which Shaharazade relates, of princes and ladies, who passed a notable part of their existence in underground palaces.

One of the chief causes of the great perturbation created by the conscription, in addition to the systematic method affected, was the deficiency of the force put at the disposal of the Sheikhs.

It was absolutely impossible for them to carry out their orders at once, even if they had not desired to turn the occasion to profit. In some places near the river, and at a great distance from the hills, however, the required number of conscripts were soon seized; but not those uniting the necessary conditions of health, strength, and a proper age. A great portion of all the first batches sent were ridiculously young, and were returned as soon as they reached the central dépôts. We saw them both arriving at Siout and departing, chained neck and neck, mere children, incapable of lifting a gun.

Our whole downward voyage was saddened by the scenes that constantly presented themselves connected with this levy of troops. At Luxor the women turned out in crowds, their faces besmeared with mud, and testified their grief by dancing the same solemn dance which they perform at their houses after a funeral. Their motions were slow, and strikingly marked; and as they threw up their arms into the air, we were forcibly reminded of certain uncouth figures of mourners painted on the walls of the ancient tombs. Indeed, our guide even, whilst drawling out such pieces of antiquarian knowledge as he possesses, "this is a boat," "this is a crocodile," "this is the inscription broken by Lepsius," suddenly stopped in the Tombs of the Kings, and pointing to a group of women, exclaimed: "These are the mourners for the conscripts!"

As soon as the batch was supposed to be complete for the districts of Luxor and Carnac, they were embarked not far from our boat. Immense files of women, in their dark dresses, came with measured shrieks along the banks, or across the fields in all directions, to mourn over the departing and curse the agents of tyranny. There was not a man among the spectators. The Sheikh-el-Beled, supported by a few fellows armed with naboots and thongs, and by a small body of Arnaouts, superintended the operation. The young men, fast bound, were led one by one along the plank, amidst the cries of the women, every moment becoming less formal, and thrilling with acuter expression through the air. At times a wave of blue dresses rolled forward, as if a rescue were about to be made; but wood and leather were brought into play, and mothers, wives, and sisters crowded back in undignified fear, tumbling, rolling in the dust; and then uprose another cursing cry, from voices shattered by grief and rage. The boat was filled to the brim, like a cart with sheep for the slaughter, and heeled over as the huge sail swelled to the wind. A last shriek of despair pursued them across the water; and the crowd broke away with sobs and tears, and forming again into long serpentine lines returned across the fields, whence they had come, tossing up their arms, and throwing right and left their wailing cries, now once again in measure, until distance, like time, swallowed up these sad sights and sounds.

Wherever we afterwards went, some fresh episode of this drama presented itself. We had not long left Gournou, for the last time, by night, when a frighful yell burst from the shore; and the words, "*Ya ibni! ya ibni!*"—"O my son! O my son!" were borne to our ears. The sounds were so unearthly that the crew at first thought it was some demon mocking them; but when our boat came opposite the mourner, he began to curse us for depriving him of his only child, mistaking us for Turks. Our people, very much alarmed—for the imprecations of a bereaved father are not launched in vain—shouted out that we were travellers, that we had nothing to do with the conscription, and begged the man to withdraw his curses. But the terrible sounds still continued—he was not to be comforted nor enlightened—and long after we had passed we still heard the same words, "*Ya ibni! ya ibni!*" alternating with denunciations against us as the supposed child-robbers.

When we came to Keneh, a most extraordinary spectacle presented itself. We had left that city bustling like a fair. The streets were filled with passengers, with pilgrims; all was life and movement. Now every shop was closed, and as we wandered along, I do not remember to have seen a single soul abroad. Some had hidden, it was said, in their houses, trusting to the inviolability of the harim; others had crossed the river, and taken refuge in the inaccessible hills above the plain of Dendera. Whenever possible, indeed, fugitives crossed to the side of the Nile facing their village, in order to be out of the jurisdiction of their Sheikhs. Some English travellers were alarmed one night by the sound of a boat-load of persons approaching their mooring-ground; and, possibly deceived by a rascally dragoman, ruthless in his cowardice, believed themselves to be attacked by robbers, and actually fired a whole broadside at the supposed enemy, which had given no signs of hostility and did not return a shot. There is every reason to suppose that the robbers were no other than conscripts—as indeed they cried out —escaping to the bank of the river opposite. Being attacked whilst in flagrant disobedience to Government, no complaint, of course, ever transpired; and it is to be hoped that darkness and the excitement of danger interfered with the aim of these doughty travellers. I mention the circumstance here, because it gives me an opportunity of remarking that fire-arms should seldom or never be regarded as weapons of offence in Egypt. If they are carried for other than sporting purposes, let it be as insignia of rank and respectability. Had a feather the same meaning it would answer the same purpose. Many young travellers come out with the idea that there are perils to be encountered; and I have seen a gentleman of this class arm himself with gun, sword, and revolvers, preparatory to taking an omnibus ride across the desert of Suez. At first sight the mania may seem harmless enough; but as long as people remain in this frame of mind, in which fear and audacity are curiously blended, they are liable to commit perpetual mistakes, and to put their own and other people's lives in jeopardy.

The aspect of Keneh, as I have already said, was indeed desolate. We could not even succeed in buying a pair of red slippers. A respectable old gentleman, who acts as English agent, received us politely, but with a gravity suited to the dismal aspect of the city. His reception-room was a little square in front of his house, where we found him sitting with a few friends, probably privileged. The windows were shut; not an eye peeped through the crevices as we rode along, driven by brats just passed the toddling period; and it was singular to see, on emerging from a bazar, where breathless silence reigned, three or four solemn-looking old men, smoking their pipes in a reverend circle, and no doubt discussing, after the imaginative manner of the Orientals, the political bearings of the events that were passing around them.

CHAPTER VIII.

Coptos — Dendera — Excursion — Haou — Bellianeh — a Pleasant Ride — Fertile Plain — Slingers — Produce of the Land — Palace of Memnon — Girgeh — Ekhmim — Traces of Ancient City — Excursion to the White Monastery — Parley with fugitive Fellâhs — Hostile Demonstrations — Immense Line of Grottoes — Athribis — The Monastery — Our Reception — Ignorant Priests — Wild Ducks — Sport — Hints to Gourmands — Meet an American Traveller — Traits of Character — Tea-Party — He feeds on Pigeons — News from our Kitchen — He goes Ahead — Canal of Souhadj — Rationale of the Inundation — the Nile does not Overflow — Alluvial Chronology — Bold Theory — Habits of the Nile.

WE had stopped at Coptos, and wandered amidst the confused ruins of the ancient city; which are only interesting as suggesting reflections, by no means new in Egypt, on the strange vicissitudes of nations. Dendera afforded us a rich treat, and being perfectly cleared out, enabled us to form a most accurate idea of what an ancient temple really was. We visited it repeatedly, and were every time more struck with its majesty and grandeur. I went alone in the evening, when the shadows were fast gathering, and found it tenanted by a few owls and numerous bats. The impression created was solemn, and will long remain on my mind.

An excursion in the desert behind the temple in search of some tombs led to no result. We started on the fourth day, and reached Haou, where we were detained until next evening by a furious contrary wind. Some pulling after dark and the following morning brought us to Bellianeh; from which place, in obedience to the guide-books, we started to visit the ruins of Abydus. It was one of the pleasantest rides I have ever taken in Egypt. The rocks of the desert, nearly perpendicular, recede here an immense distance from the river; and the fertile country reaches nearly to their feet. Soon after starting, the palm-trees are left behind, and a vast ocean of green crops, with isolated groves here and there, marking villages, stretches on either hand. The path leads through a few patches of halfé, which may be compared to barren heaths, but generally through a green lane, formed by solid masses of bean-plants, or fields of corn, or tall clover. Here and there we crossed shallow canals, dry at this season; or followed a gisr. Herons and paddy-birds were numerous; and several ichneumons darted across the path. The only sounds that disturbed the stillness of the air were the shouts of children and the clacking of slings, used to frighten the sparrows from the crops. Few men, no youths, were seen in the villages. We were told that all this fine land belongs to the fellâhs—a surprising fact, if true. It is divided into plots, as we could see by the numerous boundary-stones. A feddan is said to produce about six ardebs of wheat or eight of beans. We were puzzled in the ruined, half-buried palace, which formed the excuse for this delightful excursion, by observing that the name of one king (if all cartouches do really contain the names of kings) was in some places carefully, in others very clumsily, effaced to make room for another.

At Girgeh—like Keneh, deserted—we were again detained by north winds; but, at length, reached Ekhmim. This finely-situated town was beginning to recover from the general fright, and had possibly furnished its contingent. At any rate, many of the shops were open, and there was some bustle in the streets. We walked round the walls, over the heaps of rubbish, and amongst the small detached gardens, in search of the traces of the ancient city. They are few, and much desecrated by time and barbarism. The vast stone, which formerly overtopped a magnificent gateway, was in course of being chopped to pieces in order to be burnt for lime. The front line had already disappeared; but the others remained as when seen by Pococke. I ascertained that the additional words proposed by Letronne, in order to complete the sense, could never have existed. We did not hear, until we arrived at Souhadj, of an extraordinary monster to be seen at this place—a living child, double from the waist downwards. From the way in which it was described, I have no doubt of its existence.

From Souhadj we made another excursion of great interest—namely, to the place called the White Monastery. We did not go direct, but struck off in the first instance to the point of the hills to the south. The plain resembled that of Abydus in appearance. We reached a small brick ruin at the foot of a gorge, and intended to ascend it, to visit some tombs known to exist there. But here an obstacle presented itself. The gorge and the precipices on either side were occupied by fugitive—I was going to say, insurgent fellâhs. At first they only showed themselves sitting like crows aloft, or stealing along lofty ledges from one recess to another; but on our making an advance movement manifested a very decided intention of resistance. Some rolled down stones, others brandished spears, one or two guns; and, presently, a clacking sound preceded the fall of some very ugly pebbles not far from where we stood. The gentlemen were slinging at us; and one young rascal advanced over a spur, quite naked, and shouted to us very bravely to come on. I have no doubt they would have made good their position against a much greater force than we could have brought to bear, even if we had been disposed to dispute their right of territory. We endeavoured to parley, but to no purpose; and were fain to proceed northward, . along the base of a line of enormous perpendicular precipices. The garrison overhead moved as we moved, saluting us occasionally with a volley from their slings, just to let us know that they would stand no nonsense, and that if we were kidnappers there was no chance of catching them off their guard. We met a black, armed with a spear, driving a donkey-load of provisions in the direction of the valley, and begged him to carry our compliments to his friends.

In spite of the somewhat threatening attitude of these good folks, we climbed up to a prodigious line of small grottoes cut in the face of the rock, and generally communicating one with the other. They seem to have been used as habitations. Some old Arabic inscriptions occur here and there, and the words *παπα* and *μηνα* were written in large red characters in one of the chambers. We were warned to descend by the announcement from below that the fellâhs were growing warlike, and seemed preparing to salute our retreat with a shower of stones; so we made a regular bolt down the slope, after having seen a tomb with a Greek inscription neatly cut over the doorway. In this neighbourhood the city of Athribis is supposed to have stood.

The White Monastery, built of solid masonry, stands on the wide slip of desert between the rocks and the plain. In form it resembles the body of an ancient Egyptian temple, without propylæa or portico. Of old it had several entrances, but they are all now blocked up except one, just large enough to admit a single person. Two or three timid-looking men lingered about as we approached; but recognising us as travellers, came forward to give us welcome. We were admitted into a dark passage, narrowed from the original dimensions by massive additions of crude brick; a second gate at the end opened into a small court; and this again into a larger. Here we found the usual mud hovels built in the centre of this fine building; and a church, evidently more modern than the fortress-like exterior, but still of respectable antiquity. It is lofty, filled with quaint paintings and old Coptic inscriptions. The priests showed us an illuminated manuscript, but seemed themselves perfectly ignorant of anything beyond the present time. They could or would tell nothing; and when we found some traces of hieroglyphics on the stones built into the ramparts, or scattered about, professed never to have noticed that they were inscribed. They seemed to be in a state of great uneasiness on the subject of the conscription; for Christians, in spite of the additional tax they pay for exemption, are now seized like

Muslims. We saw only a few women, small children, and middle-aged or old men; and very probably the youths were amongst the troop that had so gallantly pelted us from the rocks of Athribis. A good portion of the ground in front of the monastery is cultivated by the Copts, an industrious people in spite of their deplorable ignorance and bigotry.

We politely declined an offer of coffee, and returned by a gisr across the fields direct to Souhadj. Here and there were ponds, in which we managed to surprise some wild ducks—very good eating. Many of the aquatic birds we shot had a very ancient fish-like smell, and an odious taste. We had seldom, indeed, much reason to be satisfied with the results of our sport in a culinary point of view, except in the case of hares, partridges, or wild pigeons. I have already recommended the last-mentioned birds to gourmands. There is a prejudice against them, and in some seasons it appears they are tough: but in January and February, stewed with onions, they make a rare dish.

It will, perhaps, be charitable to many tourists, to say a few words here on the subject of eating. I should have omitted to do so but for the following circumstance. We overtook, in descending, a small boat, bearing the American flag, and observed a portly-looking gentleman sitting solitary in front of his cabin. There was something in his posture before we could even distinguish his features that invited sociability. Two of our party, therefore—though not over-anxious, generally, to make advances—when we happened to moor near at hand, at a place called Mankabat, went on board to pay a visit. I found the traveller installed in the portico of our cabin, on my return from a long stroll. He was a lively, pleasant person, and his nationality was only sufficiently marked to be agreeable. He told us that he had the fastest horse in all America, always travelled by the fastest train, and complained humorously that he had the slowest tub on the Nile. Certainly, in spite of the size of our bark, we could have easily rowed round his sluggard. He was impatient to reach Cairo, the go-ahead impulse being strong within him, and started before us. But we soon came alongside, and, succeeding in persuading him to take tea with us, spent a pleasant evening in chatting of the

Mississippi and the Nile, the Backwoods and the Tombs of the Kings, the Rocky Mountains and the Libyan desert.

But what amused us most was, that Colonel —— (it is hardly fair to print the names of travellers one meets under such circumstances) assured us that he had eaten nothing during his two months' journey on the Nile but tame pigeons broiled! His dragoman had assured him that there were no other provisions to be procured, that beef was a myth, and that mutton was goat! We told him that at Old Cairo we had bought a leg of mutton, fourteen pounds in weight, excellent and tender; that boiled or roast mutton graced our table several times a-week; that we had procured a splendid piece of beef at Luxor; that poultry of all kinds, from geese to pullets, could be got at most places, besides hares and other game. He could scarcely believe his ears; for though, of course, he had seen flocks of sheep, and must often have been kept awake by the cackling of geese, he had been so blinded by the interested calumnies of his dragoman, that he had never ventured to go beyond broiled pigeons. The fact is, that an intelligent and honest servant will always find an ample supply of whatever is required to furnish forth a good table; and though it may be creditable to rough it when necessary, it is just as well to live pretty when it is possible to do so at a very trifling expense. Provisions are remarkably cheap on the Nile, and a price which seems amazingly small to an European leaves a good profit to the fellâh. Our American friend thanked us for our information, bade us good night when we reached Beni Mohammed, started again in his slow coach, and by persevering work night and day reached Cairo in an incredibly short space of time; so that before we arrived he was far on his way to Petra, Palmyra, or the Lord knows where!

At Souhadj is the commencement of one of the principal canals of Egypt. By its means the inundation is distributed through a vast province. It is perhaps necessary to remind the untravelled reader, that the Nile in rising does not "overflow its banks," as it is sometimes expressed; but that it filters through the country principally by means of a very complicated system of canals. The rise is first felt in the lands at the greatest distance from the river; for these are the lowest. They gradually become moist, then soften into morasses, and in some places glisten for a short time as shallow lakes. There is no rush of water along the surface; but the inundation, as it were, oozes up from the ground. Deep holes, during summer with hard-baked cracked bottoms, change slowly into wells and ponds. The fields suck up the moisture like a sponge, or are artificially gratified therewith. It is very rarely that anything like a deluge, any covering of a whole district with water, takes place; and many large tracts are never reached at all. These are chiefly near the river's banks, and are, in some cases, abandoned to the growth of halfé; whilst in others they are watered by means of the sakieh, or the shadoof. A very considerable proportion, therefore, of the Egyptian crops is produced on lands which the inundation never touches, and which depend for their fertility on unremitting human labour. Nearly the whole country, it is true, is reduced to a state of mud — even the palm-districts; but it would be very erroneous to suppose that Egypt takes a plunge-bath every year. An extraordinary inundation will sometimes bury, for a brief period, very considerable tracts, but this is quite an abnormal occurrence in most places.

Some important chronological conclusions are expected to be derived from a careful examination of a section of the Nilotic alluvium; and I have even seen it stated, if I do not mistake, that the years of Egyptian history may be counted by the strata of deposit left by succeeding inundations, as distinctly as the age of a tree may be counted by the rings of the trunk. This appears to me very bold and unsound. As long as cultivation or vegetation existed—and grass most probably sprang from the very first thin watery soil—each stratum would necessarily be blended with its predecessors. At any rate, the plough must have effectually confused this singular chronological table. Perhaps the expression I allude to may have been merely a figure of speech, intending to convey that some guess may be made at the age of alluvial Egypt, after a careful examination; but if not, it is liable to lead astray. At any rate the river, in its capricious deviations, has made perhaps as many sections as a geologist can require. I could see no sign of any series of layers apparently remaining in their original position, as annually deposited. In some places were beds of sand, several feet deep; in others, thick masses of reddish clay; in others, black mould; and if, without having any scientific knowledge on this subject, I might venture a positive opinion, I should say that from the beginning, and to a much greater extent in old times than now, man having at length acquired a certain mastery, the Nile has been a very turbulent friend, whenever he can get the upper hand—that instead of kindly spreading, year by year, a thin layer of fertile mud, he has tumbled about, and tossed up, and shaken down, out of all imaginable resemblance to an historical record, the land he has created, making islands one year and dispersing them the next, or incorporating them with the mainland, or filling up his old channel and working out another. In course of time, however, he has, himself set bounds to his own activity; and, as I have said, in many cases does not, properly speaking, overflow at all, but works underground, as fast as the Ghost in Hamlet.

CHAPTER IX.

The Serpent of Sheikh Hereedi — Episode of the Conscription — The Rock of Hereedi — Coptic Convent — Ascent of the Mountain — Expanding View — Huge Quarry — Curious Fascination — Proceed in search of the Tombs — Reach them — Sloughs of Serpents — Genesis of Saints — Living and Dead Sanctity — Sacred Idiots — Worldly Wants of Sheikhs — Remedy for Sterility — a Novel Species of Hunting — Catching a wild Saint — Mocking Disposition of the Fellâhs — Living Holiness suspected — Righteous Mendicancy — Beneficial Effect of Death — Sheikhs' Tombs — Fellâh Decorator — Rites performed at Tombs — Almsgiving — Sacrifice — Rag-offerings — Desert-tombs — Sheikh Abderrahman — Village of Raeineh.

THE story of the serpent of Sheikh Hereedi seems better known to travellers than it is to the Egyptians. At any rate we did not find any one willing to talk knowingly on the subject. This did not, however, render us less desirable to visit the tomb of the Sheikh and its neighbourhood, and we gave orders accordingly to stop at the first practicable pathway.

The mountain of Sheikh Hereedi is a huge mass of rock overhanging the river. North and south two vast semicircles of hills sweep back, leaving it a bold and conspicuous object. As we glided rapidly down towards it from Souhadj, another episode of the conscription diverted our attention. Two crowds of men and lads, harnessed to long track-ropes, were towing two huge boats against the stream, whilst several soldiers kept watch over them. They were said to be conscripts rejected at Siout, and sent back to their villages to work, and be replaced by others. Along the slopes of the distant hills we could see some of them squatting like black crows, watching this unpleasant scene.

The mass of rock that approaches nearest the river—so near that in inundation time there is no pathway left—seems separated from the rest of the mountain by a vast cleft or ravine, though in reality it is joined on by a narrow neck. Its face is pierced almost from top to bottom with the mouths of quarries, or tombs, or caves; and at one point are remains of a large building of crude brick, a Coptic convent of old times. It consisted principally of a lofty front wall, built on the edge of a terrace platform. The lateral walls abutted on the rock behind, and the inner chambers consisted of several quarries or tombs.

We moored alongside a maize-field, where the mountain recedes a little ; and climbing over a mud wall found ourselves in a lane, partly shaded by trees running along the base of the precipice. Here and there were little cells, probably inhabited of yore by hermits averse to climbing. The path led up along a steep slope, which we climbed slowly, rewarded at every step by an ever-widening prospect over the fertile plain on the other side of the river to the dim Libyan hills—dim from the excess of light that glowed round them. At length we came to a kind of dent in the upper outline of the rock, and paused to rest just below a series of vast windows in the precipice, looking out from a quarry of mighty dimensions.

Perhaps there are no such things to be seen in any other part of the world. This quarry forms a chamber several hundred feet in depth and length, with the top of the mountain for a roof, supported by pillars as big as an ordinary house. Well may the Arabs imagine it to have been one of the palaces of the giant people of old; and wonder, as they creep like insects over the floor, at the might expended in its construction. We ourselves, as we caught, at the extremity of the dim aisles, occasional glimpses of the rich plain below, or stood upon the vast sills of the windows to watch the serpentine progress of the Nile, with our cockle-shell boat just visible beneath our feet, indulged unreservedly in the admiration which the traces of power, however exerted, create; and not one of us could repress the momentary desire to take up our abode in this deserted habitation, and live for ever secluded from the world. At such times it seems as if all desires could be satisfied by the mere magnificence of the prospect; and as if it were impossible that any longing for the splendid miseries of civilised life, any desire to spring into the turbid stream that hurries a thousand to destruction for one to happiness, could disturb the contemplative existence of a hermit retired to such a cell.

But as soon as we came out again into the bracing air and the golden light, we felt once more the sting of curiosity; the fatal desire to know, to see new things and enjoy new impressions. As we entered the ravine, the jutting rocks closed in behind us, and shut out from view the valley of the Nile, so that we found ourselves surrounded with horrid crags at the summit of what appeared to be the dry bed of a cataract. Far down in a little open space we could distinguish the Sheikh's tomb glittering in the sunshine. The descent was difficult, but we effected it, and found ourselves at the bottom of a kind of rocky well.

The tomb, or rather the tombs, for there are two, one opposite the other, partially shaded by a couple of sant-trees, are little chambers with domed roofs built against recesses of the rock. The smaller one is said to belong to the son of Sheikh Hereedi. The doors were open; the floors covered with mats; but there were no signs of any recent visit. We took off our shoes and entered. In the recesses of the rock were natural crevices, where we found the sloughs of serpents, but the Arabs who accompanied us, whilst professing to know nothing of the tradition which attributes cures to the crawling guardian-demons of the place, begged us not to touch these cast-off garments. It is curious that the fellâhs of Upper Egypt believe that the slough of a serpent is good for sore eyes, and carefully preserve any they may find.

The number of persons who in every generation acquire a reputation for sanctity in Egypt is very great. Scarcely a village fails to produce from time to time a holy man, who utterly displaces his predecessor, and having gathered a tribute of solid respect during his lifetime, contrives to attract empty homage to his tomb after death. At length some other wise individual, having awakened to the profits of piety, follows his example; and thus the succession of objects of veneration is kept up. Sheer imbecility is sometimes a sufficient title to respect in the eyes of these poor barbarians, who, however, may be more prudent than we think them, and may be instinctively aware of the inconvenience of having saints too clever. The sacred idiots of Egypt, who often affect the folly which has not been vouchsafed them, are but moderately exacting in their claims. They are content to be hardly so well-dressed as the lilies of the field, provided they be required neither to toil nor to spin. Many of them, indeed, go about naked as Adam before the fall. Their cells are anything but palaces. All they require, indeed, is to be fed in idleness, and allowed to spend their lives in a state of contemplative beatitude. Now and then they vouchsafe a little advice, but oftener impart only the sacred influence which emanates from their persons. Some husbands who were in want of heirs used of old to resort to them for assistance, and the fellâhs have many ludicrous stories to relate on the subject. But it is now considered more decorous to trust to the intercession of a dead saint; although even in Alexandria, near the Rosetta gate, there is a cell where a holy man, with several deputies, is constantly, they say, employed in receiving the pious visits of wives anxious to be mothers.

It was once reported in a district towards the north of the Delta, that a strange animal—some said, a monkey of huge stature—was abroad, and did mighty damage to the crops. Many women, too, who met this thing in the fields, were frightened into premature maternity; and several men who endeavoured to catch it were severely wounded. At length the population of a great number of villages, armed with naboots, turned out for a regular battue, and succeeded in discovering their quarry sunk up to the middle in a morass. They pelted it with clods of earth until it came forth and took to the open fields, when they gave furious chase. The monster was covered with hair, but resembled a man in form. Its agility was tremendous, and for a long time it contrived to evade the grasp of those who endeavoured to seize it. However, at last, by throwing naboots and stones, the excited fellâhs managed to disable it, and to their astonishment found that it was really a human being, a raving madman, escaped from some distant village. At first they intended to finish the work they had so well begun; but some one suggested that the man was, perhaps, a great saint. They accordingly carried him in triumph, bruised and bleeding as he was, to the nearest village, where they put him in a cell, carefully barred, because he manifested a mischievous disposition at times; and ever afterwards he was honoured as a Sheikh of the first order. It is true the boys and girls of the village were often allowed to amuse themselves by tormenting him; for the fellâh has no real veneration in his character, and is ready to satirise and make fun at any moment of everything he pretends to respect—except, of course, the *deen*, his faith in the abstract, and Lord Mohammed.

The truth is, that live saints and holy men of every description are made far less of than dead ones. Shereefs, or descendants of the Prophet, have been found to be essentially rogues; and a man who has several times visited Mekka is regarded as a suspicious character. In Egypt, as elsewhere, men have discovered that holiness is a marketable article; and the whole population has suffered from the insolence of righteous mendicancy. In listening to a wandering derweesh authoritatively demanding alms, I have recognised the tones of a friar begging for his convent, or a member of a church-building society soliciting a subscription. The fellâhs, therefore, who can appreciate disinterestedness, figure to themselves a live Sheikh as a saint and a sturdy beggar joined by a hyphen; but when the forest-beard, from the depths of which alternate blessings and imprecations used to roll forth, is turned up, they forget the almost forced contributions of bread and meat, the mantle whisked by a whirlwind of prayers and menaces from off their very shoulders, the unauthorised caresses bestowed on their wives—too apt to relish the blessings of these stalwart ascetics—and, like joyful legatees, club together to build for the departed one a tomb, and cleanly to whitewash it, and gaudily to paint it, and plant a sycamore or a few acacias to shade it, and surround it with an atmosphere of respect. As I have said, these tombs remain holy only a comparatively short time, or are successively attributed to various Sheikhs. In some few cases, however, a celebrity is handed down from generation to generation, as in that of Seyid Ahmed-el-Bedawee at Tanta, and indeed elsewhere, for there are numerous cenotaphs of this Sheikh scattered up and down. The tombs in the country generally consist of a square chamber, some eight feet high, with a small cupola above, and are always white, or covered with rude representations in red ochre of camels, ships, flowers, and other objects. I remember once seeing a fellâh artist engaged in the work of decoration. He had no models, but trusted entirely to his memory or imagination; and every now and then stepped back and bent his head, first to one side and then to the other, winking his eyes alternately, and performing in fact all the manœuvres of a man of genius under observation.

The form in which respect is paid to a Sheikh who has ceased by death to be troublesome, is simple and appropriate. On some fixed day in the week the women and a few men visit the tomb, which is generally a little apart from the village, and strew palm-leaves or flowers upon or around it. They also place in some conspicuous position a few loaves of bread, or even five-fuddah pieces, often professedly for the use of his buried holiness, but in reality, by very general agreement, for that of the poor, whether of the place or travellers. The pagan custom of sacrifice is also kept up. Pious persons, either in order to obtain the accomplishment of a wish, or merely out of general solicitude for their spiritual welfare, make vows to sacrifice some animal, a sheep, a lamb, a goat, or a calf, at a particular period; and the marked victim is often allowed to pasture freely on all the lands of the village until well fattened. The feast is always public; and if there be sufficient materials, is attended by the whole population. It is also customary to tie pieces of rag and other objects to the trees that overhang the tombs — probably a remnant of the fetish worship formerly so widely prevalent in Africa.

I ought to add, that as the fertile country is covered with white-domed tombs, so is the desert dotted with little oval enclosures of loose stones about breast high, all or many of which are called Marâbuts, and indicate the last resting-place of holy men who had chosen the desert for the scene of their operations. The most celebrated of these is that of Sheikh Abderrahman, on the coast of the Mediterranean, some distance west of the Arab's Tower. I have mentioned it in the account of my visit to Siwah. It has a regular tarkeebeh, or tombstone, and is surrounded by a square court, with a wall of some height.

On leaving the tomb, or rather cell, of Sheikh Hereedi — for these places are sometimes inhabited — we still descended by a narrow steep fissure, until we came out behind the village of Raeineh, composed of houses, every one of which is crowned by a lofty dove-cote, with inclined sides — so that the village looks like a confused mass of diminutive propylæa. Returning to our boat, we started; and reached Aboutij in the evening. Next day we arrived at Siout.

CHAPTER X.

Siout—its Governor—Ismaïn Pasha—Respect of Strength among uncivilised Races — Site of Siout — the Moyeh Souhadj — Beautiful Approach from the River —A true Eastern City — Government Offices — Dismal Streets — Children at Play — the Bazar — Visit the Bath — Magnates of Siout — Egyptian Bathers — Rarity of Baths — the Barber — his Information and News — An odd Old Gentleman — Visit to the Great Cave — View from its Mouth — Wolf-mummies — Yom Allah — Master Wish — Donkey-boys — Backsheesh — Cemetery of Siout — Pleasing Scene to the Eye — Trees — The Two Lovers — Gabaneh — Ghebel-el-Koffra — the Grave-diggers — their various Avocations — Traps for Hyænas — Vultures — A Mysterious Bone — Caravan Encampment — Darfuris — Tents of Bedawins — Line of Route of the Caravan — Policy of the Darfur Government — Trade with Dongola — The Prison — A Convict's Experiences in Fazoglu — Permanent Gallows — Egyptian Jack Ketch — Punishment of Death — the Tanzimat — Torture as a means of extorting Truth — Instances — Wholesale Arrests of Servants — Soldier-police — Imitation of France — Whoever not found Innocent supposed to be Guilty.

Siout is the capital of the Saïd, although it may be said to stand only on its threshold. There the Governor, always a Turk, resides, and holds his petty court; swaying according to his good pleasure — the good pleasure of a Turk — without much interference from the authorities of Cairo, provided only the taxes come in in reasonable time, and no particular complaints be made against him. Ismaïn Pasha, who lately held this office, was violent and exacting, and yet the fellâhs looked up to him with respect, and cited with pride and admiration his exploits against the crocodiles of El-Akraat. Uncivilised races are marvellously indulgent to vigour and courage, or dexterity, in whatever way displayed; and are ever prone to exalt into demigods those who oppress them with a strong hand. It would be a mistake to suppose, for example, that Mohammed Ali, in spite of the inexorable cruelty of his government, was personally hated by the fellâhs. On the contrary, it must be confessed that they regarded him with a respectful awe which a just ruler would not, perhaps, have excited. 'T is pitiful, but 't is true. Men admire most what they understand best; and before we condemn these poor devils, let us be perfectly sure that we are not ready, every one of us, to throw an heroic halo round the first successful adventurer who conquers a throne or endeavours to filch an empire.

The city of Siout stands about a mile from the river, at the foot of a bold projection of the Libyan range, honeycombed with catacombs. A shallow canal, called the Moyeh Souhadj, drying up into detached streaks of water early in the season, passes through the narrow space between it and the desert. North and south, the hills, receding in a semicircular form, leave space for two magnificent plains to develope themselves, with their groves, fields, meadows and villages. Numerous gardens cluster round the city, allowing only the slender minarets to be seen sparkling in the ineffably clear air. The road from El-Hamra led us along a winding gisr, shaded by an avenue of trees, principally acacias of various species, some of them bearing the yellow flower called "fotn," that oppressed us with its sickening sweet smell. The low fields on either hand, still sweltering after the inundation, spread like a green lake, which the breeze ruffled into waves of changing hue, until they broke up into long silent vistas in the wooded distance. Here and there a kiosque, that hinted of siestas in the sultry noon or dreamy meditations at balmy eve;

or a tomb — where living or defunct sanctity was honoured — loomed through the distant groves, where they seemed to float, not rest. The sky was speckled with hawks, and kites, and vultures, that now swooped almost within reach, now cork-screwed upwards, until they became no bigger to the eye than larks. Here and there solitary herons were admiring their wise-looking beaks in some muddy-shored pool, or taking aim at the foolish frogs that barked insolently at them. Flights of restless paddy-birds—why may we not call them white ibises, since white they are, though not ibises?— were perpetually shifting to and fro in the plain. Along the winding tree-shaded embankments — that look like railroad causeways converted into love-lanes by a return of the Arcadian dispensation — groups of dusty fellâhs were leisurely streaming; or sleepy-eyed Bedawins, hoisted on their camels and nodding towards slumbers, which the rough brushing of leaf-laden lebek or thorny-mimosa branches alone kept off.

As we approached, it seemed really as if we had at last discovered the Eastern city of our dreams — the city where barbers are philosophers, and pastry-cooks are the sons of kings;

where Efreets may safely come disguised as woodmen, and beautiful spirits live undisturbed in wells. A massive archway of foliage led to the gate, with a raised threshold formed by a palm-tree, opening through walls over which crowd to view white houses not to be explored—and this is the great secret of the strange impression produced—but by the imagination. A humming crowd filled the first shortroofed street, where are the government offices, with sallow Coptic clerks looking through the unglazed latticed windows; and rows of naboot-armed men sitting without—constables, special or otherwise, ready to do the bidding of power. Beyond was a quiet open space, with a white tomb shaded by a sycamore; and beyond this a labyrinth of narrow lanes, with houses all turned, as it were, back outwards, and showing no sign of the life that swarms within. Most inhospitable and churlish is the aspect of these Egyptian country-towns. The streets are for the most part mere slips between dead walls, commanded by a series of high-placed loopholes. If you see an eye now and then, you do not know whether it is that of a houri, languishing and love-sick, or a robber about to take a shot at you. In other regions it is possible to catch at times a glimpse through some not too-closely-curtained window of a quiet family party, gathered at the hour of twilight round a blazing fire, or dispersed through the room, engaged in domestic avocations. But in Siout you must be content now and then to see a muffled female form crouching on a terrace, or gliding stealthily from door to door, she and her gossips only know on what errand; or a group of spindle-shanked, blear-eyed, round-bellied children, playing in a corner at the mysterious game of *Henghis Benghis, Nas Kotta Moudrias.* There is nothing else to tell you that the institution of the family — as the simplest form of society is now grandiloquently called — has any existence.

But we turn at length into the Sookh, a covered street full three feet wide from mastabah to mastabah, with little model ships, vowed offerings, like those sometimes seen in Catholic places of worship, swinging before the doors of the mosques; with shops full of merchandise and respectable Taggers; with archways leading into the balconied courts of crazy wakalahs; with donkeys, camels, and men, — perhaps one woman or girl per cent, — moving slowly to and fro, hustling, bustling, buzzing, swearing, stopping, going on; a variegated stream of turbans, tarbooshes, takyehs, and libdehs; a human beehive, a real Arabian Night's bazar, where we are as much out of place as a Chinese in the High Street of an English provincial capital. We went to the bath to be sweated, and scraped, and rubbed, and lathered, and soused, in company with the respectabilities of Siout—brown-skinned, hairy, pot-bellied gentlemen, who submitted to the operation with a gravity and sedateness at once admirable and ludicrous. Our presence, perhaps, put them upon stilts; but it was evident that, as they lay like porpoises about on the slushed benches, enjoying a gentle titillation from the horny palm of the bath servant, or submitting head, back, and breast to the cunning razor, they felt what important people they were—citizens of a place which possessed a real bath, with hararah, faskiyeh, and above all, a scalding Makhtas—the *summum bonum* of the Egyptian bather; for not all the race of Pharaoh bathe, as not all Frenchmen go to cafés, nor all Englishmen to clubs. From Cairo to Siout we had not found one of these luxurious establishments; Manfaloot, which now washes cold, not hot, having been deprived of its bath by the greedy river. Girgeh and Keneh, and one other place, I believe, are alone equally fortunate with Siout.

The barber whose assistance we requested was a hugely sagacious fellow, with seventeen hairs on his chin, which he boasted had never felt the razor. He had travelled as far as Manfaloot, and had heard that at Cairo were five hundred palaces, three hundred mosques, and two hundred baths. He had heard likewise that the English came down to the mighty sea in ships, that the Muscovites were as numerous as flies in Egypt — hyperbolical barber! this was said to astonish the natives — that the French had chosen Sultanah Horeeyeh — which being interpreted, is Queen Liberty — to rule over them. A variety of other interesting facts were buzzing about the uninhabited regions of this shaver's head; but we could not stay to hear all his stories. In the ante-chamber, whilst we were being kneaded, as if for dough, by a coaxing lawingee, one old gentleman, who had doubtless been soaking for hours, came and sat down, wrapped in a sheet, opposite to us, and looked with simple astonishment in our faces. At length he murmured, "Where is the country you come from? — where, where? Where are the ships that brought you?—where, where?" We thought he wanted to enter into conversation; but on our speaking, he went on with his murmured soliloquy: "Fain, fain; where, where?" It was evident that he knew perfectly well; but he had been suddenly impressed with the vast distance we must have travelled to come to that place, and when we left, he was still rocking himself to and fro in his sheet, and murmuring in his philosophical and inquiring mood, "Where, where?"

During our first stay we visited, of course, the great cavernous tomb, palace, or temple, which yawns in the side of the hill above the city; and wandering through its vast halls, enjoyed those impressions of grandeur in search of which our countrymen — supposed to be so unpoetical — travel thousands of miles. Little else but impressions, however, can be gathered. The sombre walls are covered, loaded with inscriptions; but who can read, who can understand them? A stratum of dirt and rubbish encumbers the floor. Here and there, openings that slant downwards tell of further subterranean chambers; but they are all choked, except one in the inner room, which seems to descend zig-zagging. No one has explored them, I believe, in recent times; but as far as all experience goes, treasure-seekers have been more industrious than searchers after historical truth, and have left their traces everywhere.

Sitting down on some stones at the mouth of the cave, whilst discussing the advisability of exploring the thousand other openings in the face of the mountain, we gazed on the bright green plain with its islands of palm-groves, and the serpent river showing its shiny scales here and there. A scare-crow donkey-boy who was with us, being learned in the tastes of travellers, brought out some grinning wolf-mummies, and broke them up in search of the scorpions that are often found therein; but another, more unsophisticated, reproached him, saying, that it was a sin to violate the last sleep even of a dead dog; and that corpses, both of beasts and men, should be left in peace even to the day of Judgment. (*Yom Allah!*) This scrupulous lad was named Tolbeh, the "Wish," because his mother had longed for a son, and had made a covenant with the Almighty, that if her desire was gratified she would call her child by that name. He was of a mild, effeminate character, a phenomenon among donkey-boys; but if I remember aright, he was only temporarily engaged in the business.

Donkey-boys at Siout get one-third of the receipts for themselves, over and above the usual backsheesh, which travellers, totally misunderstanding the usages of the country, are beginning to refuse. Little do they imagine that for the sake of a penny present, which custom makes due after a hard day's work, they get themselves placed on a level with ruffianly Arnaouts or bulliragging Greeks.

Instead of poking amidst a succession of dusty tombs, the diminished proportions of which would have smoothed away the impression of grandeur we had received, we descended the rugged hill, and leaving the bridge leading back to the city, over the Souhadj Water, to our right, entered the long narrow cemetery which has been established between the base of the mountains and the extreme limit of the inundation. It is difficult to imagine a more softly pleasing scene. The tombs, which are really elegant little white houses, with domed roofs and arched doorways, and gardens surrounded by scollop-edged walls, form a perfect street, with masses of trees breaking in here and there upon its long perspective. The common acacia, the mimosa gummifera, the fotneh, all thin-leaved, cluster into groves that cannot conceal the domes beyond; the giant sycamore spreads its solid shade over the road; and the lebek and the palm rear their contrasted forms side by side. In one of the tombs we were told in a whisper, as if it were some unnatural crime, two lovers had been buried, side by side, in the same cell, not even separated by a partition; and Oriental prudery, speaking by the mouth of Tolbeh, represented them as having been reduced to a heap of black cinders. In Muslim countries the sexes are kept asunder even in death, and women's tombs are preserved from profane eyes as scrupulously as the harim.

The cemetery is called Gabaneh, and the mountain that overlooks it Ghebel el Koffra—the "Mountain of the Gravediggers." These men are said to form a peculiar tribe, which has lived from time immemorial among the tombs, or in the caves above. Their office, besides that of preparing the last homes of the worthy people of Siout, is to keep watch night and day, in order to protect the handsome grave-clothes sometimes used from the cupidity of body-snatching fellâhs. They are not, it seems, always successful—perhaps they are not trustworthy; and corpses, carried away entire, are sometimes found at a distance, stripped of their rich shawls and embroidered anteries. The Koffra pursue a variety of avocations in order to eke out their living. Among other things, in Ramadhan time they go up into the mountains and set traps for hyænas. The tinkling of a bell announces when the game is caught; and they forthwith beat the unfortunate brutes into humility, and then take them, muzzled, round the city and the various villages of the district, to exhibit them for the amusement of the fellâhs.

Beyond the fashionable cemetery is the grave-ground of the poor. As we clattered through it a number of huge unwieldy rakhams, or vultures, went away in short flights, resting at every ten yards. The fatness of these loathsome creatures, that looked at us with epicure eyes from beneath their bald, wrinkled scalps, seemed to me of suspicious origin, especially when I remembered the thin covering of earth sprinkled over the departed Muslim. At any rate, they perform admirably the office of scavengers; and for this, as well perhaps as because they may have eaten their fathers, are respected by the fellâhs. It is a popular opinion that one of their bones—no one knows which—has the extraordinary property of swimming against the stream; but, few being ever killed, this strange bone has never yet been found.

We came at length to the encampment of the caravan from Darfur. It had arrived two months back, and was now (December) much reduced in numbers. Most of the slaves, with their masters, had gone on to Cairo; but there was still a good deal of merchandise, especially heaps of senna, on the ground. The Darfuris, black and surly, declined to talk, and looked at us askance. A good many Bedawin tents, belonging to the escort, were scattered here and there; but the chief part of those who had not lodgings in town lived in little sheds formed by two heaps of bales, or leathern camel-bags, with mantles or blankets spread across. The usual time occupied in performing the journey from Siout to Darfur is two months, passing by the oasis of El-Khargeh. Formerly a much more expeditious route across the desert was open; namely, from Dongola, which province exported a considerable quantity of dhourra. But the Darfur government, fearing the encroaching disposition of

Egypt, have, within the present century, closed this route, forbidding any one to use it on pain of death, and compelling commerce to adopt exclusively the tedious and dangerous route from Siout. Their object is to isolate their country as much as possible, even more than their national traditions justify, because they anticipate an attempt at least at conquest. Lately, as an additional security against the ambitious dynasty of Cavalla, the Sultan has declared himself the most humble servant of the Porte, and voluntarily pays tribute; but he has by no means raised the quarantine in which all the upper provinces of the Egyptian empire are placed, and Dongola still suffers from the loss of its only profitable market.

During our first visit we passed by the prison, and saw a number of melancholy-looking men sitting in front of it. On asking who they might be, we were told that they were the fathers of a number of young conscripts, at that time confined in the prison, and intended for Fazoglu; but probably they were the relations of criminals destined for transportation to that abhorred region. I once saw a man who had performed the journey on compulsion for stealing a book from the mosque of the prophet Daniel in Alexandria. He had come back an honest man, having expiated his crime. Sad was the account he gave of his adventures, and well fitted to produce in all listeners the morality that can be inspired by fear. Soon after passing Essouan, he said, there was no bread to be got; people ate maize soaked in water—frequently grains of corn found in the excrements of beasts; their wolfish eyes were ever glaring round for something to devour. This description more particularly applied, he said, to Fazoglu itself; and may be correct enough, if restricted to the convict miners, who are not likely to be very tenderly treated.

A permanent gallows—grim and horrid object—stands in an open space outside the walls to the south of the city; and children, in its intervals of leisure, play at bo-peep behind the worm-eaten timbers. The gallows in Egypt is a pillory for a corpse, the criminal's neck being always broken by the executioner before he is slung up. It is to be observed that the office of John Ketch, though it may invest its incumbent with terror in the East, inspires no disgust; and the man who whips off a head or breaks a neck with a piece of old rope and a stick, may nevertheless be regarded as, and for that very reason may be, an excellent citizen. I have my doubts about the expediency of the absolute and unconditional abolition of the punishment of death; but I must confess that the abhorrence and hatred which the humble instrument of justice excites in all classes, high and low, without exception, is a terrible condemnation of the system. Society seems delighted to find a scape-goat for the sin it commits.

I have already alluded, in speaking of the Tanzimat, to the difficult question of capital punishments in Egypt—pointing out that it is almost useless to interdict formal condemnations to death as long as the naboot system is tolerated. To perish by the cord or to perish by the stick seems to me all one, except that the second method is more painful. I may here insist on the fact, for the benefit of those who still talk of civilisation in Egypt, that it is the every-day rule to apply *torture* to elicit confessions of guilt from supposed criminals. There is a famous instance in which one of the Pasha's Wakeels, pompously styled Minister of Foreign Affairs by Europeans, applied gravely to the English Consulate for six sailors, charged very unjustly with murder, in order that they might be made to plead guilty by the application of the stick and other means. This very year in which I write (1852), a case has come to my knowledge, in which a man under suspicion of robbery, stoutly asserting his innocence, was in the city of Alexandria, where European influence ought to act if anywhere, actually hung up by one finger of each hand for a considerable time; and as, after this terrible ordeal, he persisted in his denial, they let him go maimed, naïvely observing, that he might be falsely accused!

If a robbery take place in a European house it is the habit to accuse the servants, at least of complicity—though in general this class of men are far honester than their fellows in Europe—and a whole establishment, with the addition sometimes of relatives and friends, is sent to the Pashagah's, there to be dealt with according to the custom of the country: that is to say, to be beaten once or twice a-day for a week or so, until they cry *peccavi.* It is unpleasant to admit that few native masters go to this extremity, experience having perhaps taught them that servants are generally suspected unjustly. However, it is the rule, without previous examination, upon simple surmise, to beat and rack suspected persons; and, indeed, to suppose that every one who is arrested must be guilty. As in France, the army is degraded into a police; and when I go along the streets of Paris, and see four or five fierce-looking chasseurs escorting, with fixed bayonets, some drunken tramper or obstreporous chiffonnier, I am reminded of the not very exaggerated caricature of the system in Alexandria. There a group of savages in uniform may sometimes be seen, as they drag a prisoner along, to beat him with the butt-ends of their guns, as a preliminary punishment; and if the delinquency charged be a personal outrage, or even a debt, the plaintiff is often there, taking out his vengeance beforehand, as a security against the possible caprices of justice. "I knew he would be discharged," quoth a *bourgeois* of Abu-l-Abbas; "but I had the satisfaction of breaking his teeth and knocking out his eye!" A man who had stolen a melon, was once killed in attempting to escape; but this horrid circumstance has also its sanction in Europe—I mean in Paris, which is the same thing: for there, not six months ago, a person arrested for some trifling offence, choosing to run away, was deliberately shot down by his guard, and Public Opinion, as it read the circumstance in the morning-papers, shrugged its shoulders, and said, "*Ma foi, c'était la consigne!*"

CHAPTER XI.

Visit to the Caves of Dronka — Recruiters again — Coptic Cemetery — Convents on the Face of the Rock — Vast Quarry — A Wolf — Ancient Hermitage — Crushed Chapel — Giant Beehives — Unfinished Excavation — Emme Bey — Ride to Mankabat — Keerawans — Indolent Sportsman — Market-day at Manfaloot — Tel-el-Amarna — Local Modifications of Religion — Difficulty of reading Hieroglyphics — Reason of presumed Failure — French Flippancy — Failure of Philologists — Reasons — Jumping to a Conclusion — Hasty Criticism — Tomb of Sheikh Seid — Dead Saint's Servants — Sheikh Abâdeh — Ancient Coins — Drainage — An exiled Courtier — Village of Rauda — Forced Labour — Mode of Payment — Truck System — Ashmounein — Watchman — Discharged Soldier — Punctuality — Aversion to Military Life — Fellâhs timid — Mode of carrying on a Quarrel — Vain Threats — Brutality — Reason why the Army is disliked — Magical Effect of Pay — French Dislike of Military Life — Tombs of Beni Hassan — Art of viewing Antiquities — Glass-blowers — Catacombs — Impertinence of Tourists — Arab Scrawls — Evening Approach to Minieh — Moonlight — Object of Travelling in Egypt.

In descending the river towards Siout we had observed, both with the naked eye and the telescope, a long series of cave-entrances in the face of the rocks to the south of the city. We resolved, accordingly, to visit and examine them. Crossing the canal, we proceeded for some distance along the base of the mountains, in which the innumerable tombs of ancient Lycopolis are excavated, and came to the village of Dronka. By this time the rocks had receded a great distance from the river (at Siout they reach within a mile), leaving a vast plain and a considerable extent of desert slope. As usual, at the mouths of the ravines we saw crowds of patient fugitives sitting on the look-out for their enemies, and here and there in the plain below were stationed equally patient recruiters armed with naboots, engaged in the agreeable process of starving their brethren into submission.

At Dronka is a Coptic monastery, and near it the cemetery of that people. The tombs, oblong and rounded at top, are formed of small bricks, some black, some white, arranged like the squares on a chess-board, and look neat and pretty. Beyond the village there is an immense line of precipices, from the base of which descends a long slope, cut up with innumerable gulleys. We kept near the edge of the cultivated land, reserving a minute exploration for our return. With the exception of an excavation at the bottom of one of the gulleys, having a kind of portico in front, all the caves were on the same line. Near some of them were very large crude brick buildings, apparently clinging to the face of the rock. These were inhabited Coptic convents, round the doors of which two or three men lingered, watching our progress very attentively, as if doubtful of our peaceable intentions.

At length we reached a considerable ravine, not winding gradually to the plain, but terminating in an abrupt precipice, as if there had once been a fall of water there. On the hill beyond was a vast cave, which I visited. It was a quarry—perhaps the most extensive in Egypt—the roof supported, as usual, by immense pillars cut out of the rock. I went as far as I could see; but at one point darkness prevented me from proceeding. As I wandered along the aisles, I saw a wolf cross a patch of light, no doubt in a state of great indignation at being disturbed. At the entrance of the quarry is a line of vast stones, some twenty feet long, and about fifteen feet high. I at first thought they had been cut of that size for removal; but it is more probable that they have fallen by their own weight.

Returning to the foot of the ravine, we found traces of a staircase leading up nearly to the summit of the rock. It terminated in a series of small caves and chambers, artificial and partially covered with stucco. They had probably been inhabited by a hermit. At this point commences a ledge along the face of the rock, leading to the entrances of all the quarries and to the convents. We visited them, therefore, in succession. The former exactly resembled the one I have already described, except that they were somewhat smaller. The convents were built against the entrance of some of these excavations; and in one instance a very large chapel had been fitted up in the rock of yore, but a vast mass of stone had fallen in and crushed it to atoms. The people were civil, and offered us araki. Near their habitation other colonies were established; namely, of wild bees. Their hives or nests were built against the surface of the rock, projecting perhaps only two feet, but covering a space twenty or thirty feet in diameter. We passed through the thousands that came out, as if disturbed by our voices, with some uneasiness, but without any accident.

The excavation I have mentioned, as being faced by a portico with six pillars, is unfinished, and may have been intended for a temple or a tomb. About it are some small niches, in one of which we saw an ugly statue. During the whole of this excursion we did not discover a single inscription or see the trace of an hieroglyphic. We returned, however, well pleased, to our boat at El-Hamra. This may be called the port of Siout. It is a small village, but has often one distinguished inhabitant, namely, Emme Bey, the French governor of the little oasis of Farafrah. The boats are moored along a bank shaded by a handsome avenue of trees.

On leaving Siout, we told our reis to go round to Mankabat, resolving to ride thither on donkeys. The road is pleasant, especially the first half, through a succession of gardens and groves. Among the acacias of Waladieh we shot some keerawans, which proved to be excellent eating. At Mankabat are large sluice-gates, by which the supply of water is regulated during the inundation. On an elevation above one of the ponds in its neighbourhood was built a kubbeh, or little domed summer-house, as we would say, formerly used by some wealthy Turk as an ambush from which to take aim at the various kinds of water-fowl, which in the season repair thither. Reclining on cushions, with pipe in hand and gun across his knees, the lazy sportsman used to watch his prey from the arched windows, and every now and then bring down some fishy ducks or worthless ghatteys. I waited some time on fortune in the now ruined summer-house, but the pool attracted nothing but huge cormorants and a few sly ducks that kept on the other side.

Taking boat, we proceeded to Beni Mahommed, and having spent a morning there went down to Manfaloot. It was market-day when we arrived, and all the paths of the neighbourhood were covered with Bedawins, mounted on camels or horses, and dressed out in their best. We were told that in a village not far off the fellâhs, instead of flying to the hills, had resisted the conscription by main force, defending themselves in their houses with guns and spears.

At Tel-el-Amarna, which we reached next day, are some interesting brick ruins, and still more interesting tombs. The main feature of the representations on their walls is a star, shooting forth rays that terminate in hands. What appears to me very weak criticism refers these monuments to strangers; but it is more probable that we do not yet know all the local modifications which the religion of Egypt underwent. The inscriptions that would explain the symbolic representations, if they could be read, are in hieroglyphics; and, as I have already taken occasion to observe, I remain sceptical as to the power of our scholars to obtain any satisfactory information from such inscriptions. The reason of their want of success seems to me, apart from the difficulty of the subject, their impatience to be complete. There is nothing so painful as the reconstruction of a broken sentence, even of a language we know. To set aside Greek and Latin, we cannot make sense even of some of our own dramatists; and a learned editor of Jonson, in the vain attempt to clear up everything, is absolutely reduced in his irritation to blackguard a whole series of predecessors. And yet the hieroglyphists pretend to derive information—contradictory to all plain written documents, to the testimony of eye-witnesses; mere foolish Greeks, it is true—from inscriptions in a language of which they know neither the roots, nor the construction, nor even the whole alphabet. When I was learning Greek and had got as far as my omicron, I should have been ashamed to contradict Moses on the authority of a passage that included all the letters to omega. But our modern decipherers are not so modest; and poor Champollion, who discovered a *faute d'orthographe* in some Thothmean tablet, is still a type of the school—as Dr. Lepsius, who *will* write in characters he cannot read, is the exaggeration.

After all, is it well proved that every one of the signs which are used apparently to construct a word possesses a phonetic value? I doubt it, when I am shown some twenty distinct forms of the same letter. At any rate, I doubt that the powers of those forms can be ascertained without a previous knowledge of the ancient Egyptian language. I do not believe there ever has or ever will be an instance in which an unknown language, written in an unknown character, has been deciphered; so that, even with the assistance of the Rosetta stone, the lucubrations of hieroglyphists seem to me not to have risen much above the level of the commentaries on *Jack Stiles, his mark.* When they attempt to write in plain English letters a sentence which they have worked out of their stubborn mine, it is amazing that the bewildering unreality of the syllables—the absolute impossibility of giving them sound with mortal lips—the utter hopelessness, without grammar or dictionary or tradition, of extracting a *proved* meaning, does not drive them to despair. Yet, no—they do not despair; but, jumping very wisely over all these threshold difficulties, gravely discuss the unextracted kernel of their nut—facts, theological, moral, scientific, whimsical, historical, philosophical. It is true that Champollion, with the intrepidity of a Frenchman, invented a thresher's song in the tombs of Beni Hassan; but he had previously invented a grammar and a dictionary. His successors have abandoned the philological department, or at any rate keep the result of their studies to themselves; for be it remarked that hieroglyphists in general claim to be as oracular as the inscriptions they expound, and though the reasons of their translations be as plenty as blackberries, will not give them except on compulsion. I once saw a man in a madhouse, standing opposite an old chair without a lever and without a fulcrum, and yet fancying himself to be Archimedes moving the world. He reminded me of Mr. Blank poring over the tablets of Abydus, and constructing systems of ancient Egyptian history and chronology.

A little below Tel-el-Amarna, among some steep rocks, is the tomb of Sheikh Seid. As we passed it, a number of large white birds—hundreds of them—like kites, came flying round us, almost brushing our rigging. Our boatmen thought we were going to fire at them, and interceded earnestly to prevent us. These birds, they said, were the servants of the Sheikh, ever on the wing around in search of food for him. It was the custom of passing boats to give them bread. We broke up a couple of loaves; and sure enough each bird as it caught a piece went away in the direction of the tomb. The flight followed us only a short way, and having picked up the last crumbs from the waters returned to the rocks.

Our next halting-place was at Sheikh Abâdeh, where we of course visited the remains of the town. Among other things we noticed the extensive system of drains, a refinement apparently unknown to the Pharaonic race. In the vast mounds of rubbish, money, coins, and small relics of antiquity are still found; and a dozen girls crowded round the boat, vociferously insisting that we should buy, and we contrived to amuse ourselves for half an hour by bargaining. Mixed with the coins were small square pieces of glass, fragments of mosaic work, which were peculiar from their having a thick layer of gilding just below their surface.

Among the ruins strolled a handsome young Turk, who seemed a favourite with the children of the place. We afterwards learned that he was a Memlook, or servant of the Pasha, sent up to the sugar-factory opposite, as to a place of exile, for some trifling offence. The punishment may be considered light by some, but to one accustomed to bask in the beams of princely favour, and to strut or ride about the busy streets of Cairo, I have no doubt it was very dreadful. In all countries there seems to be an inexplicable fascination about a court, so that whosoever once flutters there cannot be distanced without misery. I am disposed to think, that in that atmosphere men exercise qualities of little use or value in other circles, and find themselves in the ordinary relations of life as much at a loss as if they had passed through the hands of the Coptic priests of Siout: but a question thus delicate requires a more competent judge. At any rate the exiled lord or slave of the bed-chamber, whom we saw at Antinoopolis, had the vacant and unhappy look of a hound that misses the daily cuff and caress of its absent master.

Opposite Sheikh Abâdeh is the village of Rauda, with a large sugar-estate and factory, occupying some thirteen hundred men. Of course all these poor people are forced to work for wages arbitrarily fixed. They are nominally paid twenty-five paras, about three-halfpence a-day; but this they never get in hard cash. The truck system is carried out in the most relentless manner, and the unfortunate devils (from whom a heavy percentage is re-exacted in the shape of taxation) are paid in the refuse of the molasses calculated at a good price, and after the owner of the factory, one of the Cavalla family, has deluged the market with his produce. Of course this is almost equivalent to not paying at all. The men are said partly to live by stealing, partly by means of little allotments of land left to them, which they cultivate at night. I ought to add, that there is nothing peculiarly atrocious in the character of the owner of this estate, nor are the above circumstances uncommon in Egypt. They are the rule, not the exception; and, after all, why should we be indignant? These barbarians merely carry out, in a brutal straightforward manner, the idea which is at the bottom of all our political economy; namely, that the real workers of this world are entitled to only just sufficient salary to keep off actual starvation. I sympathise with a square-headed, broad-paunched, belching Turk, wielding sword and koorbash, to compel a whole district to administer to his ferocious appetites, far more than with a delicate perfumed philosopher, who can sit down calmly and discuss the principles of supply and demand, according to which society developes or narrows the proportions of that stupid thing called labour.

We went to Ashmounein, some distance inland from Rauda; but although the ride was pleasant and interesting, nothing occurred worth recording. I saw a large serpent among the mounds, at least six feet long. A man, to whom I spoke, was there as a kind of watchman. He told me he had been in the Morea under Ibrahim Pasha. This was the only old soldier discharged I ever met in Egypt; and even he was still employed by one of the governing family. The idea of punctuality had been strongly developed in him by fear and military discipline, so that even the hope of a present—which will usually keep a fellâh at your heels until evening, because what you give him can scarcely be less than a day's wages—could not induce the veteran to serve me as a guide beyond a certain hour, at which he had some stated duty to perform. As a rule, these men, once taken, never return and mix with the population, which partly accounts for the aversion felt for a military life. "I would rather," said a fellâha woman, "see my son dead at my feet, than that he should be taken as a soldier; for then I should at least know where his bones lay."

It cannot be said that the fellâhs are a particularly courageous people, although good soldiers have been made out of them. As a rule, indeed, they are rather timid; and, like all nations south of England and Germany, are valiant in gusts, and more from fear or self-love than virtue. It is amusing to see two gigantic men engaged in a quarrel that would at once be decided by fisticuffs in our pugilistic latitude. The party aggrieved, or considering himself so, holds on by the garments of the other, uttering unintelligible cries and threats, and the following dialogue generally takes place :—

"Will you let me go?"

"No, I will not, Wallah!"

"If you do not let me go, I will break your teeth, Wallah!"

"I will not let go, Wallah!"

After about half an hour, the person held, probably feeling that he ought to go to work, makes a show of hitting the other, who only hangs on the tighter and yells louder. Then the bystanders interfere, saying, "*Maellesh! maellesh!*"—"It is no matter;" words that seem to have a magical power, and are also used as synonymous to "I beg your pardon," if you tread on a stranger's corn. A reconciliation is effected easily enough, if the disputants be of about equal weight; but I have seen a big man beat a youth very savagely for persisting in holding on to his gown. It is to be observed, however, that this is considered a very disgraceful act; for as long as the hand remains clasped the victim is supposed to be under the protection of his enemy. This, perhaps, accounts satisfactorily for the immense number of threats that are expended in vain in these quarrels. According to rule, you must free your coat tail by artifice or gentle violence before you hit.

Thus Egyptian quarrels generally evaporate in words. I ought to add, that among the very low classes of the towns, the donkey-owners and inferior tradespeople, a good deal of brutality is exhibited towards boys not big enough to defend themselves; and it is, no doubt, their example that knowing travellers imitate when they lay into sailors and servants. Perhaps the fellâhs can scarcely be called cruel; they are not deliberately so at any rate, but, like all timid races, might easily be excited into committing very atrocious acts. They are often very unmerciful to their beasts, and I have seen camels the objects of the most savage inhumanity.

But it is not from cowardice that the Arabs object to serving in the army. It is simply, as I have elsewhere noticed, from the fact that they do not receive sufficient remuneration for their services. Although they certainly cling with a good deal of affection to their native place, they are not by any means a stay-at-home people. Perhaps this tendency to roam has been created by the oppression to which they are subjected, and they roll about beneath the superincumbent weight like corn-grains endeavouring to escape from the inexorable millstone. However this may be, fair hopes of reward will lure them anywhere, whether there be danger or not. We induced two donkey-boys to undertake the traject of the Libyan Desert, to them peopled with unimaginable terrors. Dragomans go yearly to Syria, and Sinai, and Petra, because there is a reasonable chance of return; and I have no doubt that any European power could levy willing armies amongst the fellâhs. The Egyptian Government takes its men by force, and pays them, or professes to pay them, twenty paras a-day, equivalent to five farthings. Perhaps this is enough, if regularly paid, to support life, where provisions are so cheap; but something more would be required as an inducement. Every one knows that in France, the military nation *par excellence*, to be taken as a soldier is considered one of the unlucky chances of life, against which people insure as against fire or shipwreck, and even seek the assistance of sorcery; and no doubt one of the principal reasons of this is the prospect of seven years of semi-starvation, only to be alleviated by a war, or by gratuities that must have a corrupting influence.

In our ascending voyage we had passed in front of the tombs of Beni Hassan, impelled by a strong wind, and had put off the necessary visit to those curious places. By so doing we had reserved a rich treat for ourselves. These tombs are situated in the face of a ridge of precipitous hills that advance almost to the river. They are all cut out of the same stratum of rock, so that the doorways extend in a long horizontal line, visible even from the opposite bank of the Nile. We went carefully over them all. Their chief interest consists in the numerous minute representations that cover the walls, of circumstances connected with the domestic and agricultural life of the ancient Egyptians. Nearly all we know on these subjects is thence derived; and if we could read the inscriptions that accompany the drawings, we might probably know enough. As usual in these monuments, there is not the slightest trace of artistic feeling. The outlines are stiff, though firm; and the colouring is flat, not even pretending to imitate nature. There is more promise in the daubs that decorate the Coptic churches. But the Egyptian paintings are not without merit of a peculiar kind. There is an obstinate adherence to conventional truth, and it is nearly always possible for a practised eye to make out what is meant. In one of the tombs of Upper Egypt I remember seeing a group of men sitting, with long tubes extending from their mouths to the ground. My first impression was that they were smoking, but my guide-book tells me that they represent glass-blowers, and I yield to the decision of superior experience. But this, and a thousand other similar mistakes that a novice is liable to commit, proves how feebly the Egyptian understood or practised the mimetic art.

These tombs, as they are called, were more properly speaking chapels, the real place of interment being in catacombs beneath, communicated with by square wells, and in some instances by staircases. Most probably they were visited for pious purposes at stated periods, by the families to which they belonged. The Arabs look upon them as palaces of some gigantic race destroyed. I am sorry to say that the pestilent habit of covering ancient monuments with modern impertinences has been pursued here to a most extravagant extent. One gentleman seems to have gone to the trouble and expense of erecting a scaffolding, in order to daub his name in colossal letters of pitch upon a ceiling. The Arabs have been at work, too; but, singular to say, have chosen for the perpetration of their marine subjects, interlarded with sentences from the Korân, a chamber where little or no traces of ancient painting remained.

Leaving Beni Hassan we rowed for Minieh, along unruffled reaches that soon shone silvery beneath the rays of a full moon. Our crew, as was their wont in pleasant weather, chanted cheerfully as they pulled, but not continuously; for at every stanza they paused that the men of our companion-boat, that glided nearer the bank, might take up the song and send its notes thrilling back over the waters. Such evenings form delightful stations on the backward road of memory; and when I linger over them, and the measured splash of the oars, and the tinkling of the dripping shower between, and the intricate quavers in which they praised the City of the Imam, come again to my ears; and when the river, like a more brilliant atmosphere beneath, full of dim forms and dazzling specks, and the shadowy shores in the distance, and the gliding boats here and there, and the illuminated heavens; and when at length the white kiosques, and slim minarets, and massive groves of Minieh seen by that light, which shows only a dreamy outline and quenches all deformity in its glow;—when all these sights and sounds group themselves into a tremulous picture that a breath may blow away, it seems for a time that life can be life only in Egypt, and that Sorrow can be rocked to sleep nowhere so well as on the Nile.

Many other places were visited by us during our descent towards Cairo; for whilst all hoped to perform the journey again at some future period, yet, considering the uncertainty of human life, we determined to become as well acquainted with the country as possible whilst we were about it. I will not, however, enumerate our stoppages, nor describe our many excursions, although my memory lingers willingly among those scenes. Perhaps I have already dilated too much in the narrative way. My desire was by a series of small pictures, incidents of manners, and anecdotes, to fill up certain lacunes in the great outline, which a host of previous travellers have sketched, of one of the most singular countries and peoples on the face of the earth. I am scarcely satisfied with my success. Egypt, in spite of its apparent uniformity, when seen from a distance, presents a myriad facets on nearer inspection. There is much to learn of human nature by observing it; and for this reason I have cared to trace its paths, and glide over its waters, rather as a student of manners than as an antiquary. Generally speaking, travellers have looked upon it as a Museum. I look upon it as one of the compartments of this present world, in which a not unamiable family of my fellow creatures fight the eternal fight of life and joy against suffering and death.

CHAPTER XII.

Associations of the Nile — The River-God — Feeling of the Fellâhs — Sub-fluvial Affairs — Watery Kingdoms — Course of the Nile — Inundation — Canals — Mud of the Nile — Use of the Wind — Equivocal Generation — Fish — Vagaries of the River — Mountain of the Birds — Optical Illusions — Trees — The Lebek — Christian Traditions — Aspect of Egypt — No scattered Houses — Fields and Roads deserted at Night — Wandering Demons — Uses of Superstition — River at Night — Night Sounds — Strong Light of the Stars — Clouds — Thievery in Egypt — Habits of Sailors — Number of Boats on the Nile — Various Forms — Grain-boats of Siout — Steamers — The Go-ahead System — Boat travelling — A timely Protest —Variations in Depth of the Nile — The Railway again — The Two Lines — Political Lucubrations — No Demand for a Railway — How will it pay? — Rates of Freight—The Project condemnable—Regulations that have been laid down — Mode of supplying Rations — Deserters — Do Railways make Traffic?—Nothing new under the Sun — The Barrage of Karakoush.

A PARTING word for the Nile. There is verily no name in the world which awakens more numerous and more touching associations. Other rivers may be old, geologically speaking; but this is *the* old river of history, and no one who has been a schoolboy, or has felt the Bible leaves flutter beneath his hand, can be without some affection for it, some yearning to behold its rolling waters, some anxiety to know of its manners and appearance. The Egyptians, especially the fellâhs, have a deep veneration for the Nile; and although they are called an ungrateful nation, are not so in this instance. In spite of their monotheism, of modern origin, I suspect they have a latent belief that their river is a God, and it requires all the inexorability of their Mahommedanism to prevent their paying him divine honours. Their saying, that whoever has tasted once the waters of the Nile will desire to taste them again, is well known, and means something more than that the draught is wholesome and good. They have singular things to tell of sub-fluvial affairs, and know the precise situations of the capitals of many extraordinary realms. The King of the Fishes holds his court in one place; the King of the Crocodiles in another; whilst near the Rosetta mouth is the country of the Mermen, who now and then catch a human being and show him about in a cage, carefully pointing out to the grinning populace of the watery regions that the strange animal has got no tail!

I have not materials to give a complete history of the Nile, or I would introduce it here in despite of my plan. All I wish to do is to add some few touches to the notices already scattered up and down these pages. I know nothing of it beyond the first Cataracts. From thence to the sea, as every reader is aware, it grows beautifully less, receiving not one drop of water, save the dews of night and a few insignificant showers; whilst it is drawn upon throughout its whole course, by means of canals and machines, more or less primitive, for the irrigation of the country, which otherwise would soon be parched into a desert. During the autumn inundation, as I have already said, the country is not converted into a lake; but immense bodies of water, partly by means of canals, partly by means of filtration, are, as it were, mixed up with the greater portion of the cultivable lands, reducing them to a state of mud, or covering them with shiny patches like the fragments of a huge shattered mirror. The canals are generally shallow at the mouth, so that as soon as the

Nile sinks a little, all communication with it is shut off. Their course is almost always near the desert parallel with the river, and at many points they are traversed by solid bridges of limestone. The principal ones are the Moyeh Souhadj and the Bahr Yusuf on the western side; but innumerable others, of less importance, are ready to suck in the rising inundation and prevent the disasters that would otherwise be inevitable.

It is worth observing, that while the Arabs attribute great fertilising power to the muddy deposit of the inundation, they also lay much stress on the soil which they believe to be brought to them by the wind. The stronger the tempest, say they, the richer the crop. Possibly the sand, which is sifted over the country by the wind, may be useful in qualifying the excessive fatness of the mould. But I believe that there is no especial virtue in the mud of the Nile; and that in fact the waters carry their load but a short distance, comparatively, every season. It is common, however, to speak as if once a-year Egypt received an entire fresh layer of soil from Abyssinia. As is well known, any tract of land, however sandy, irrigated during a very brief space of time, becomes fertile; so that whilst other countries labour painfully to increase their surface by draining fens and reclaiming salt-marshes, Egypt has nothing to do but to sprinkle water over the desert to make it bring forth harvests. The Arabs, by the way, believe that insects and reptiles of all descriptions have been produced, according to the doctrine of equivocal generation, from the slime of the Nile; and that man himself, under the hand of the Almighty Artist, developed into beauty and life from the same ignoble material. In inundation time the pools and lakes with which the country is covered teem with a peculiar species of fish, of small size, but very delicate to eat. The fellâhs pretend that they are created by the warmth of the sun at that particular season; but they are found at other periods, though rarely.

Like all rivers running through a country composed of yielding materials, the Nile frequently changes its course at certain places, eating away its banks, breaking through promontories, creating islands, or leaving them to join with the mainland. Half the town of Manfaloot has been devoured in this way, and many villages are on the verge of the stream one season, and far inland the next. In some places the river runs through the centre of the plain between elevated banks, from which there is a gradual slope down on either hand to the desert; but its tendency is to seek one side or the other, and it often crosses diagonally from the rocks on the western to those on the eastern bank, keeping, however, in preference, to the latter.

From Silsilis downwards, I do not think it once absolutely touches the Libyan Desert, whilst in many cases it washes for miles the base of the eastern hills. The precipices at Ghebel Aboofeyda, Ghebel et-Teyr, and elsewhere, rise like vast walls with a level summit above the pigmy boat as it glides along, and may be seen covered with myriads of black cormorants and other aquatic birds, that can just find footing on little ledges or projections, whence one of the above names.

When the Nile does not hug the precipices, some singular optical illusions are produced. All the eminences on the plains of Egypt are insignificant and artificial, and the slightest mound, therefore, forms quite a feature, and is eagerly sought by the eye. Thus at Edfou the lofty rubbish heaps, crowned by two tall propylæa, are seen at many miles' distance, and are magnified into giant proportions; and the walls of Sa-el-Haggar, far removed from all objects of comparison, seem, when first they rise above the horizon, to be perfect mountains. A village, built on the accumulated ruins of huts of other times, easily acquires to the eye the dimensions of a feudal fortress; and the cupola of a Sheikh's tomb may be mistaken for the dome of a cathedral.

A good many trees sometimes unite their forms to produce groups of singular beauty; and various species of the mimosa, the sycamore, the lebek, the orange, and the citron-tree adorn the neighbourhoods of some of the large towns. But, generally, the vegetation is distributed in uniform masses. Immense groves of mimosa, the wood of which, cut into the shape of bricks, is used in boat-building—a classical reminiscence—occur near Siout; the sycamore is the favourite tree in some regions, the doom in others; but the palm, congregated in groves of varying extent, sometimes almost meriting the name of forests, is, of course, the favourite tree. It is far more beautiful, however, when seen alone, or rising above clumps of drooping branches, shot out by pillars that have only just started from the ground, than in vast masses; but it is always an ornament to the landscape.

One of the trees above-mentioned, the lebek, calls to mind some very learned controversies. It is simply a species of mimosa, remarkable for casting a very dense and agreeable shade; but it bears the name of another tree, which is said to have disappeared some five hundred years past, and to have been identical with the Persea of the ancients—the poison-bearer that became a food-bearer by being transplanted to the kindly soil of Egypt. There used formerly to be shown, near the city of Ashmounein, the lebek under which Mary once suckled the infant Saviour, and a whole grove that prostrated itself in adoration when he approached. But these Christian traditions are becoming rarer of late in Egypt. In describing a lady of perfect stature, the Arabs now say "like a palm;" formerly they said, "like a lebek."

From the boat Egypt looks like two hedges, or rather like an avenue of groves and woods, with distant mountains seen through the breaks. When you land, the aspect changes to a sea of green dotted with tree-islands. The villages are rarely visible from afar off, being buried in trees; the cities are, for the most part, surrounded by gardens, and show only their lofty minarets. Scattered houses there are none, as in other countries; no villas, no châteaux, no wayside inns—nothing but a few rare sheds, composed of four sticks and a handful of green reeds, built by the labourers as a temporary retreat from the sun. The towns, villages, and hamlets are scattered at regular distances—a malaga, or Egyptian elastic mile, apart; so that whilst by day the fields teem with life, there is no intermediate station for a traveller, no chance of meeting a single person abroad after dark. At sunset the fellâh, unless engaged in night-work, invariably seeks his home; he would consider himself a most miserable man if compelled to move alone after that hour. Sometimes he affects fear of robbers; but what should those gentry do abroad in the bean-fields, or on the gisrs, when all honest men are at home? The real reason is that devils choose that hour to walk abroad, assuming all sorts of alluring or terrific shapes. Even during the short twilight these dreaded beings begin their wanderings, often under the form of a white hare or a white ass, as I once had ocular proof on my return from the Pyramids of Ghizeh. Foolish, therefore, would be the fellâh who would venture, except from motives of strong interest, to put himself in their way. Even the villages, however, are often visited by devils or ginns, under divers forms, as cats and camels, giving good or evil fortune, according to their treatment or their capricious tempers, like our fairies. When a fellâh from any cause omits to say his evening prayers, he is safe to dream of devils and to pass an unquiet night. In all countries humble people forge enemies or friends for themselves in the invisible world; and this is, perhaps, the only way in which their minds can be prepared for sublimer affirmations and more important doctrines. The uses of superstition are somewhat misunderstood in these matter-of-fact days, when men are prone to measure heaven with a compass and to weigh imponderable spirit.

But if the plains are deserted as soon as night sets in, not so the river. True, a great number of boats, those especially that are breasting the current, seek the bank, and moor, if possible, in the close neighbourhood of a village, under the care of its dogs and its naboot-armed watchmen. But others continue their course; and when the moon gives light, and the wind still serves, it is almost always possible to see one or two pale sails stealing along. In calm weather boats continue to row or float until a late hour; and to the usual night-sounds, the gurgling of the stream, the splash of a leaping fish, the dive of a marauding rat, the barking of dogs, are often added the plaintive voices of a still labouring crew, singing of beauty and love, or the throbbing notes of the darabukah.

I have noticed in Egypt, but not elsewhere, that trees and sails are sometimes reflected in the stream by the light of the stars. These luminaries in that latitude and in that clear atmosphere are, indeed, of extraordinary lustre; and as they melt and expand their radiance in the smooth waters, seem to deprive night of half its gloom. Rarely is a vault of impenetrable vapour built up between the world and them, but a semi-transparent veil dims them occasionally; and in spring great processions of scattered clouds migrate, like birds of passage, towards the mountains of Abyssinia.

When a traveller's boat is moored near a village, one of the crew is deputed to keep guard, for petty larceny is sometimes apprehended. At a few places it is the custom to fear robbery on a more majestic scale, and one or more paid watchmen are hired for the night. These precautions, generally excused by some old tradition of violence, are chiefly taken in Middle Egypt; and as such is the rule, it is better to comply with it than to keep your reis and crew, timid fellâhs for the most part, in a state of trepidation. Of late years, however, nothing like an attack has ever been perpetrated; and for our own parts we did not lose the value of a piastre.

The crew, unless tired by a very hard day's work, generally sit up until a late hour, wrapped in their mantles or crowded round a large fire. When there is a coffee-house open, some few of the most dissipated repair thither; but the majority abstain, and amuse themselves, as I have said, with story-telling, or grave conversation, or pleasantry, as their mood may be. Generally speaking, instead of warming like a parcel of grog-drinking Europeans into boisterous merriment, they became more serious as the night waxed old, and as the coffee and the pipes began to tell upon them.

It has been calculated that there are five thousand boats, small and great, upon the Nile. This is, perhaps, over the mark, but the number is certainly very great. In Upper Egypt the peasants use a triangular raft made of reeds, about six feet long and four broad at the base. On this they lie breast down, when for any purpose they wish to cross to the opposite bank or go to work upon an island. The next step from this primitive simplicity is the little punt, carrying one man and impelled by a sail some three or four feet square. Then follows a long series of various kinds of boats, up to the dahabieh, a hundred feet long and twelve broad at the beam. Siout possesses a small fleet of grain-ships of even much larger dimensions, capable of containing five thousand ardebs. A good many small steamers ply between Cairo and Atfeh, and pay occasional visits to the upper country. It has lately been proposed to run a steamer every season as far as Thebes, for the convenience of travellers. All great things with which men meddle have their attendant follies. The distinctive characteristic of the present age is progress, movement; and I have certainly nothing to say against this. But vulgar minds always exaggerate; and because it is good to be in motion, would convert life into a treadmill. The *beau-idéal* of the go-ahead gentlemen is, to be shot round the world in a cannon-ball; and I have no doubt, if people could come the Captain Cook in this diligent way, they would believe themselves to be highly improved by their travels. "I've been, and sure I ought to know," would be in every mouth, and the flood of misconceptions, worse than ignorance, poured into society, would be enormous. Of course those who go to Egypt merely for the sake of amusement, have a perfect right to forego all the delights of boat-travelling — liberty, comfort, and profitable idleness; and to cram themselves into a small steamer, in which, without beds, unless they pay enormously, and with a certainty of Irish stew twice a-day, they will be remorselessly hurried forward to their destination, allowed half-a-week of exploration, and then be returned in a state of bewilderment to Shepheard's Hotel. I advise, however, those who would really enjoy and understand Egypt, to use the dahabieh, as I would advise the camel or the ass for the desert, the sledge for Lapland, or the diligence for France; and I protest beforehand against all octavo volumes on the manners, institutions, and antiquities of Egypt, written after the adoption of the electric style of travelling.

The Nile varies in depth, not only in every season, but at the same place from year to year; and its navigation requires, therefore, considerable skill and attention. In spite of all efforts boats do often run aground. Generally they are got off without much difficulty by the united efforts of the crew, whilst steamers remain sticking for thirty hours or so, and frequently require to be tugged off.

I am almost afraid of being mistaken for a Conservative, for after having, as a matter of sentiment, objected to steaming tours on the Nile, I am going, as a matter of humanity, to return to my criticism on the proposed railway. As a question of English policy I have always advocated a railway from Cairo to Suez, but on the express understanding that it should be executed with English capital and by free labour. Many of the arguments and facts I brought forward in a series of papers on that subject, are now used with singular inaptness in favour of the railway between Cairo and Alexandria. The two projects are totally different in scope and character. The first would have been highly advantageous to Indian travellers, and would, I think, have paid as a commercial speculation; the second will not be particularly useful for the transit, and will, I believe, not pay, at least for the present. The first was an English idea, conceived purely as an improvement on the present clumsy and disagreeable mode of crossing the desert; the second is a French plan, intended to unite the fortified port of Alexandria with the capital; and the Macchiavels of Paris are delighted that, by a singular mistake, we should thus prepare the way for an occupation which they now consider as inevitable.

For my own part I do not lay much stress on the political speculations to which this railroad has given rise, and I should be sorry to see Egypt kept in a backward state by the fears and jealousies of great powers. But, as I have already said, it is a mistake to suppose that railroads are the apostles of civilisation. They are the effect, not the cause, of modern progress—

just as the abolition of armies will be the effect, not the cause, of a wide-spread love of peace. There is no particular demand at present for a more rapid communication between Cairo and Alexandria. The number of travellers, exclusive of Indians, is absolutely not sufficient to pay for a steamer once a-week. Indeed every purpose is served by the vessels moved to and fro in preparation for the fortnightly transits. Those, therefore, who look to profit, must depend on produce, and must calculate that the government will close the locks of Atfeh, and *force* the people to bring their cotton, their clover, and their beans, to the terminus at Cairo. Unless this prove to be the case, it is ridiculous to suppose that boats, after having performed a journey of three or four hundred miles, perhaps in a month, will go to the expense of transhipment and railroad rates to save a few extra days. I believe it is now admitted in England that bulky articles—coal, for example—can always be carried cheaper by water than by rail. Why should not the same be the case in Egypt, especially as there the stuff to be transported is produced over a vast extent of country, and will have to pay almost the same freight to be carried to the terminus as now to Alexandria? The difference between the cost of conveying corn from Siout, for example, to Cairo, and from the same place to Alexandria, is comparatively trifling, because the distance and time saved in the first case is not sufficient to enable a boat to make an extra voyage in the season.

On economical reasons, therefore, there is no ground to be enthusiastic in favour of this project, which is highly condemnable in a moral point of view. In these days, when our outlying land alone is struck and gilded by the last rays of freedom slowly setting towards another hemisphere, I should like to see Englishmen, instead of being carried away by hopes of profit, or by a mania for locomotion in the abstract, rather chary of suggesting fresh means of oppression to prince or pasha. I do not think that the present Viceroy has any disposition to be a tyrant. He wields the authority he has received with some moderation, and has at any rate invented nothing new to torment the people, except the conscription, which I really believe was meant by him for a reform. But he has not yet had the desire or the courage to emancipate the fellâhs; and if he be persuaded that such and such a work—a railroad, for example—be useful and desirable, he will, of course, think it no sin to carry it out according to the custom of the country.

That I may not be suspected of yielding to ungrounded fears in respect to the way in which the railroad works are to be carried out, it is as well to mention the precise regulations which it seems have been laid down. The engineering department is contracted for by an Englishman; and the rails are supplied by us, as by the cheapest market. But all the rough work is to be carried out by the Egyptian Government—by means, of course, of forced labour. The men required are taken wherever they can be found; and are nominally paid a piastre a-day, and supplied with rations. I say nominally, because if these promises be strictly carried out it will be the first time to my knowledge in the history of Egyptian public works. The labourers were to be supplied with rice during the execution of the canal, but in consequence of some misunderstanding between the divans of Cairo and Alexandria, which were to send provisions on alternate weeks, were more than once left to famish; and every kind of payment of salary is always in arrears, a year or eighteen months at least. That the labourers themselves are not satisfied may be inferred from the fact, that already strings of deserters have been seen marched in chains into the streets of Alexandria; and this alone is sufficient to convince me that we have done a very foolish and discreditable act in forcing on by advice, or other means, the construction of this railway. Now it is commenced, let us hope it will prosper; but I confess to having strong doubts on the subject. It is no longer, I believe, admitted as a principle that railroads make traffic, at least in any perceptible degree — any more than canals make water; and none of our prosperous lines would ever have been laid down had not the previously existing means of conveyance been successful as a speculation.

Another great public work, with which Englishmen happily have had nothing to do, is the Barrage, intended to bring about an improvement on the inundation. As yet it has only succeeded in obstructing the river — to say nothing of the sufferings of those employed to construct it, and the immense sums of money wasted on engineers and machines of all kinds. The French are very proud to attribute the invention of this large idea to their mythological hero, Napoleon; but they do not know that he was only the plagiarist of a Turk, styled "ignorant and rash" by the traveller, Abd-el-Latif, six hundred years ago. There was a bridge of more than forty arches at Ghizeh, built by the Eunuch Karakoush, in Saladin's time, from the materials of various small pyramids. These arches were closed by the superintendent in order to throw the inundation over the plain; but the river at once asserted its right of way, and began the demolition of the bridge. The same accident will probably happen if any attempt is ever made to use the Barrage for the purpose for which it was intended.

CHAPTER XIII.

Threat against Egypt—Bahr Bela Ma—Importance of the Inundation — Means of Prognostication — The Drop — Curious Superstitions — Partial Failures — Famines — Intercession of Heaven — History of a Bad Inundation— Terrible Effects — Famine — Pestilence — Cannibalism — Eating Children — Strange Gourmands —Punishment — Adventure of a Physician — A Lady Cannibal — Immense Mortality — Desolation of the Villages — Emigration — Repeated Disasters in succeeding years.

A THREAT, of atrocious sublimity, was once directed against Egypt—the casting of the stream of the Nile through an artificial channel into the Red Sea; and the consequent reduction of the country in the space of a single season to the condition of a gigantic Bahr Bela Ma, or River without Water, such as that which winds over the Libyan desert. The realisation of such a threat is by no means physically impossible, but the infernal energy necessary to carry it out is almost unimaginable. We may suppose, therefore, that to the end of time, unless some frightful natural convulsion intervene, Egypt will continue to profit by the annual inundation of the river.

As the prosperity of the country is known to depend on a few cubits more or less of water, the habits of the Nile have naturally been observed with great assiduity by the people all along its banks. Various systems of prognostication have been invented, and are yearly resorted to, though none of them seem to be very correct in their result. Nearly all the women on a particular night comply with the practice I have already mentioned, of placing a piece of dough or clay, on the roofs of the houses, and many without any other object than to ascertain whether the inundation will be copious. They assume that if the lump increases in weight, which it does by absorbing the dew, the quickening drop, the generating Nukta, has fallen. Observation, however, may have shown them the fallacy of the predictions thus obtained; and yet, instead of giving up the practice, they continue it with another object—that of ascertaining their chances of life and death, or general good fortune. The superstition is derived from the Copts, and was no doubt rife under the Pharaohs.

In other houses, about a pound of mould is placed in a vase with an equal weight of water; and as men always contrive to cheat themselves into hoping, evil is expected only in case the mould absorbs the very last drop of water. Others figure the twelve months by paper boxes filled with barley grains, and are satisfied if one of them increase in weight; others derive comfort from divers intricate arithmetical calculations; and some examine the condition of the dates and the quality of the honey produced by the wild bees. The colour of the water during the summer months, and the various changes it undergoes, require more careful observations, but seem to give a far more correct result. The fellâhs here excel their ingenious brethren of the towns, and their predictions of good or evil seem often to receive confirmation.

Partial failures of the inundation occur from time to time, attended with more or less misery. Within this century, famine has more than once threatened the country. On one occasion, when the water delayed many weeks to rise, there was a perfect panic; and the Pasha thought proper, as a last resource, to beg for the intercession of Heaven. Being somewhat doubtful as to what church, sect, or form of faith enjoyed most favour on high, he determined that all should offer up prayers on the same day. Accordingly, ulemas, muftis, priests, rabbis, the representatives of all forms and modifications of religion, went down to the side of the river, to supplicate for the all-important rise, which in due season took place; and was attributed by Muslims, Christians, and Jews, to the special efficacy of their prayers.

History has preserved the record of one horrible visitation, by which Egypt was afflicted. In the year 1199 (596 of the Flight) various indications had forewarned the people that misfortune was impending, although none dreamed of the extent to which their sufferings would reach. During May, June, and July, the waters of the river became green and fetid, and full of worms and other inhabitants of stagnant pools. They began to rise slowly in June; but by the middle of September had not attained more than twelve cubits, instead of the eighteen required as a minimum. The rains had failed in Abyssinia: and the greater part of the lands of Egypt remained parched beneath the sun.

"In this state of things," says the traveller, Abd-el-Latif, who sometimes reminds one of Boccaccio, "the year 597 (beginning in October) approached like a monster that threatened to destroy all the resources of life, every means of subsistence. There was no longer any hope of an additional rise; the prices of provisions were already exorbitant; the provinces withered beneath the drought; the people foresaw an inevitable famine, and expressed their fear by tumultuous movements; the fellâhs left their villages, and took refuge in the great towns; many emigrated to Syria, to the Maghreb, the Hejaz and Yemen, dispersing like the children of Saba, when the dykes of Mareb gave way. An immense number flocked to the cities of Misr and Cairo, where a frightful famine and pestilence received and devoured them; for when the sun entered the sign of the ram, the air putrified and the plague began its ravages: and yet the poor, urged by famine, fed upon carrion, human corpses, dogs, and offal. They soon indeed fell to devouring children, and it then became a common occurrence to seize wretches who had roasted or boiled infants in their possession.

The Wali condemned those who committed this crime to be burned alive."

In this abrupt way does Abd-el-Latif present to the mind at once all the horrors which he is about to describe in detail. He then seems to copy from his journal, as he had set them down, a variety of instances of cannibalism. The victims were at first always children; very often killed and devoured by their own parents, who argued that it was better that they should eat them than others. Children could not be allowed to go abroad; for sometimes they were seized by men or women made wolfish by hunger, and devoured on the spot, or carried away to be prepared for the table in some infernal kitchen.

"When the poor began to eat human flesh, the wonder and horror excited were such, that these crimes were in every mouth, and people were never weary of the extraordinary topic; but by degrees custom operated, and produced even a taste for such detestable repasts. Many men made children their ordinary food, eating them from pure gluttony, and laying up store of their flesh. Various modes of cooking and seasoning this kind of food were invented; and the practice soon spread through the provinces, so that there was not a single district in which cannibalism became not common. By this time the practice excited no surprise; the horror it at first excited entirely vanished, and the matter was discussed as quite common and indifferent, Divers rich people, who could have procured other food, seemed to become infatuated, and practised cannibalism as a luxury. They had murderers for their purveyors, and invited their friends to dinner, without taking too much trouble to conceal the truth.

"Children of rich and poor, abandoned by their parents who had fled, filled the streets and bye-places like locusts that have lighted on a plain. The hungry watched them from their concealment, and suddenly rushing forth pounced upon such as they had selected, and carried them away. The police in vain endeavoured to check the practice and arrest the criminals. They rarely succeeded in seizing any but women. Of these, thirty were burned at Misr within a few days, all confessing to have eaten more than one infant. I saw one taken before the magistrate, with a roasted child hung round her neck. They gave her two hundred blows to extract a confession, without obtaining any answer. She seemed to have lost all the faculties of human nature. As they dragged her violently away, she expired on the spot. It always happened that those who were burned one day were found devoured the next, the flesh remaining being well-cooked!"

By degrees it was no longer merely children that fell victims. Grown men, those especially who were distinguished by corpulence, at length found it necessary to be on their guard.

"A physician was called by a man he knew to a house in the great street. This man, as he walked along, gave alms of some small pieces of money, and recited certain words of the Korân, that seemed to imply that he required forgiveness. This circumstance aroused his suspicions, and he began to fear he was falling into a trap. However, the good opinion he had of the man, and the desire of gain, combated his suspicions, and he suffered himself to be led into a large half-ruined mansion. Here his conductor was met by a stranger, who, not seeing the physician, said,—'Having tarried so long, let us hope you have brought some fat victim.' Upon this the physician leaped out of the window, and lighted fortunately in a stable that belonged to an honest man, who told him that it was well known the people of the neighbouring house made a practice of decoying men, to kill and eat them."

An instance is given of a great lady, who was attracted by a savoury smell rising from some huts under the windows of her palace, and desired to taste of the mess. She was gratified, and learned that it was composed of human flesh. Instead of feeling any horror, she forthwith employed her poor neighbours to steal children for her. "The constant use," says Abd-el-Latif, "of such food having made her very ferocious, and inspired her with inclinations exactly resembling those of carnivorous beasts, her serving-women, fearing she would at last devour them, denounced her. She was arrested, but her rank, and the circumstance of her being with child, protected her from punishment.

"As to the number of the poor that perished of hunger, God only can count them. I can testify that at Misr, at Cairo, and the neighbouring places, it was impossible to cast one's eyes around, without perceiving many dead or dying persons lying about. From Cairo alone, from one to five hundred corpses were taken out to be buried daily; and at Misr, the number that perished was so great that it was impossible to remove them, and the bodies were allowed to remain and encumber the streets.

" As to the suburbs and the villages, all their inhabitants perished, with the exception of a very small proportion. Only the chief cities of the provinces retained even the semblance of a population. A traveller would often reach a whole village in which not a single person remained alive. There were dead bodies in every house. We entered one village, and found not a living soul. In the interior of the houses, the condition in which the people were found exactly illustrated this passage of the Korân, in which God says,—'We have reaped them and exterminated them.' The whole family was there,—husband, wife, children. In another place, where had been four hundred weavers' looms, the same spectacle presented itself. We saw the weaver lying beside his instruments, and his whole house lifeless around him. In many places the wolves and hyænas had come down, and were feasting on the dead. The river was covered with floating corpses.

" The route from Egypt to Syria was like a vast field sown with human corpses; or rather like a plain in which the sickle had been at work. It had been changed into a banqueting-hall for birds of prey and for wild beasts; and those who had taken their dogs as companions and guards were devoured by them. This emigration scattered the Egyptians over the face of the earth; and it was observed that mothers even abandoned their children, that they might be less encumbered on their way. Add to this, that freemen and freewomen were sold as slaves, even with their own consent; daughters and sons, by their parents; and libertines satisfied their passions to satiety for a few wretched coins.

"In fine, as I have said, the greater part of the towns and villages were left without inhabitants. Misr was almost entirely depopulated. Many streets and quarters remained without a living soul; and those that still lived used the wood of the deserted houses for fuel."

The Nile, meanwhile, began to sink considerably. The Nilometer was left dry; islands appeared in the river covered with ruins of ancient buildings; the waters again corrupted. In fact, all the phenomena of the previous year were repeated; and when autumn came again, the river barely rose to the height of fifteen cubits and a half, so that only some districts felt its benefit. It seemed as if Egypt had been visited only by the phantom of preceding inundations—like those spectres that appear in dreams, and vanish at once. This year there was a terrible earthquake, that was felt throughout all the adjoining countries, and did prodigious damage. The misery of the people continued, but less in degree, for they were less in number; and the practice of cannibalism had almost entirely ceased. The third year, again, the inundation threatened to fail; and an impression went abroad that something extraordinary had happened at the sources of the Nile, and that Egypt was about to be reduced to a desert. But at length the waters came down "in mountains," and all drooping hearts were revived. The land was soon again clothed in green, and the miseries that had been endured became a tradition.

Such, in substance, is the account given by Abd-el-Latif, an eye-witness, of one of the most terrible calamities that had ever afflicted Egypt. I may here add, that there is little doubt that in former times the inundation was more complete than it is at the present day, the general surface of the country having risen. It is true that the bed of the river has risen likewise, but probably not in the same proportion. It would seem that what are now called the Sharaki lands, that is, such as are never covered by the waters, received that name formerly only in some years when they were left dry by the operation, as was supposed, of the east wind. I do not know what proportion of the country is now Sharaki, and what Rei, or annually inundated. Mr. Lane, whose testimony is of the greatest possible weight, tells us that the chief portion is Rei; and I have usually assumed his statement to be correct. Possibly it applies to the land actually cultivated in the present depopulated state of the country (the government of Mohammed Ali was nearly as disastrous as a bad inundation); for it is generally admitted that at least one-third of the available land is now absolutely abandoned; and this, added to the Sharaki districts yearly utilised, would perhaps equal them to one-half of the entire surface of the country.

CHAPTER XIV.

Illustrations of Fellâh Manners from Fiction — Town Story-tellers — Fellâh Story-tellers — The Tantawi —Anecdote of the Horned King — Story of Hak Hak.

I SHALL now introduce one or two stories, which, though of course fictions, may be taken as illustrations of fellâh manners, because they seem to proceed from fellâh minds. The professed story-tellers of the cities rarely place the scene of their romantic fictions in the country. To them, what we call a pastoral is almost unknown; and as soon as they get beyond the walls of Cairo, at one bound reach the region of the marvellous and the supernatural. An Efreet is always hanging about in the suburbs, to carry to some distant city an unfortunate hero, who is invariably chosen from among the intramural population. The story-tellers love to dwell on the adventures of sons of kings, of politic ministers, of wealthy merchants, of shopkeepers, artizans, water-carriers, and even ass-drivers; but they disdain to waste the efforts of their imagination upon anything of fellâh, or rather of country origin. They are probably wise in thus restricting themselves to topics which are familiar to them, even at the expense of losing the great advantage of variety of incident and scenery. They endeavour, however, to make up by luxurious descriptions of artificial gardens for the absence of those magnificent glimpses of real nature which the vast plains of their native land would afford.

The truth is, the citizens of Cairo and Alexandria always look upon a villager in a ludicrous point of view. They are acquainted with none of his qualities but his ignorance, his simplicity, his poverty, and the slavish condition in which he is kept. Whenever, therefore, the story-tellers introduce him, it is in the character of a clown, malicious without wit, and continually subject to buffetings and dupery. "If the lion could paint, where would the man be?" have I often thought, in a moment of exaggerated sympathy with these poor outcast fellâhs, seriously to ask anything very remarkable from whom, in the way of intellectual exertion, would indeed be mere irony. They are an honest, serviceable race of men; they will do anything for you within the limits of their comprehension; but, in truth, those clever rogues the Caireens, in the selfish pride of their accidental superiority, are not so very far wrong in their judgment.

However, the fellâhs are not absolutely dumb. They have something to say for themselves—not very elegant, not very creditable, perhaps—but still something. I went once to the Pyramids of Ghizeh with a Frenchman, who had had the original idea of taking a fellâh servant, a grown man from Tanta. As a matter of course, the other servants, and even the ass-drivers, made a butt of this poor fellâh, whom they christened Tantawi, putting all the work upon his shoulders, and making fun of him into the bargain. He took this treatment tolerably well, breaking out into imprecations and expostulations, just sufficiently to tell that he was aware what they were at, but submitting in the end with commendable patience. During a halt we made, one of the most impudent of our lads, after a good deal of miscellaneous teazing, said that he knew a capital story of a Tantawi, or Tanta man; and being called upon to relate, spoke nearly as follows:—

"In ancient times there lived a king named Iskender, who had two horns, of which he was so ashamed that he hid them under his turban, and never uncovered his head except to his barber, who was both deaf and dumb. For many years he reigned without the secret being discovered; but happening once to make a progress through his dominions, he stopped at Tanta, and feeling his head itch, desired to get shaved. So he called for the court barber, but found that that day both his hands were hindered by paralysis. Feeling his head itch more and more, he at length made up his mind to get a man from the village, and to secure his silence by menace of death. He was shaved, therefore, and dismissed the Tantawi barber with a handsome present, and the promise that if he divulged what he saw he should be impaled.

"The man ran away, putting the money in his mouth; so there was no danger he should unlock his teeth to tell anything until he got home. When in his own shop, however, he felt the secret distending his stomach, and he knew for certain he could not keep it in. So, after cutting the heads of half-a-dozen customers, he closed his shop, and ran out into the fields to look for some quiet place where he might pronounce the three words that were on the tip of his tongue. He stopped first in a grove of trees, and seeing nobody near, was about to speak, when a great flight of crows came and settled over-head.

"'Who knows?' thought he: 'the king may be in communication with the birds.'

"So he left the grove, and went into a wide open field; but here there were goats and sheep, and he was afraid to open his lips. He proceeded a little farther, the secret still swelling within him, like an ostrich's egg in the breast of a sparrow; and met a friend, who asked where he was going. He tried to answer; but only three words presented themselves, and these were his sentence of death. He rushed away like a madman, holding his hand before his mouth, until he came to a water-wheel working in a deep well. The buffaloes were going round—round—round; the water fell splash—splash—splash; and the wheel groaned *nein—nein—nein*. The boy had fallen asleep under a tree close by, with the goad in his hand.

"Then the barber cautiously climbed down the well, even to the water's edge, and crouching as if to drink, whispered to a large frog that came up to stare stupidly at him—'*Iskender-loo 'ornein*' (Iskender has two horns). Immediately he heard the wheel overhead take up his words—'*Iskender-loo 'ornein—nein—nein—nein.*' He was so bewildered that he was afraid to move; but remained there trembling like one palsied for several hours; whilst all the while the buffaloes went sleepily round—round—round; the water fell on his back—splash—splash—splash; and his creaking confidant repeated the burden of his confession—'*Nein—nein—nein.*'

"Now it happened that the king had been disturbed in his mind since the morning, lest the secret of his deformity should be revealed by the barber. So he walked through the village to see if the people were laughing one to the other; but he observed nothing unusual. He went forth into the fields with his attendants, repeating to himself the very words which the barber had used; until he came to a long fence of reeds, through which the wind was whispering—'*Ein—ein—ein.*' Whereupon he knew that the truth had been told in that neighbourhood;

and proceeding a little farther, reached the place where the buffaloes were going round—round—round; and the water fell splash — splash — splash; and the wheel groaned *nein—nein—nein.* The boy, seeing the king approach, had thrown away his goad and climbed into the tree; so that when they searched they found nobody, until they looked down into the well and saw the barber.

" 'Seize the dog!' cried the king, in a rage, when he recognised him; 'seize him, and let him be impaled!'

" And thereupon, said the narrator, without the slightest compunction at concluding a ludicrous anecdote with so tragic an incident, the Tantawi barber was accordingly impaled!"

Great was the merriment which this absurd story excited, and for a moment I thought that the Tantawi was perfectly overwhelmed. He frowned, he blushed, he grinned, and did his best to appear unconcerned. It was evident, however, that he was hurt at hearing a native of his village thus held up to ridicule. A more ready wit would have turned the tables at once; and, like provincials nearer home, would have represented some citizen of the capital in a laughable situation. But the poor Tantawi was incapable of this, and seemed only to aim at proving that his village did not monopolise all the simplicity and stupidity of the country. At any rate, this was the point of his narrative, inasmuch as it was an answer to the attack made upon him. Probably, like a thousand similar ones, it was originally constructed with the object of satisfying that spirit of depreciation in which peasants are apt to indulge towards their neighbours. As to the audience, they naturally did not choose to take it as a confutation, but rather as a confirmation of their theory, and laughed as heartily at the story-teller as at the story. Much, indeed, of the drollery consisted in the tone in which it was expressed, and the gestures by which it was translated and annotated; so much, that I almost fear to find the reader incredulous, when I say that all the hearers, ourselves included, rolled on the turf in ecstasies of laughter as the snuffling Tantawi proceeded with his narrative.

"Know that about four malagas from the town of Tanta there is a village called Kafr Hemmir, the Village of Asses. It is inhabited by a people so stupid that they cannot count their own feet, and always call to prayers two hours before noon, lest they should be too late. Formerly, they were still more stupid; and it is said that once, when their Mueddin had a sore throat, they lay in bed all day, because they did not believe the sun had risen.

"About that time there lived amongst them a youth who was hump-backed. He had been found by one of the women under a palm-tree asleep; and as she could not guess how he came there, she supposed he must have been brought by the birds. So she called to them, asking what was his story; but the crows replied, 'Caw, caw;' and the sparrows, 'Chip, chip, chip;' and the doves, 'Coo-hoo-hoo.' Then the poor woman sat down by the sleeping hunchback and said:—

"'Little crooked thing, didst thou come hither of thy own accord, or wert thou brought by a camel, a horse, a buffalo, or an ass? Awake and speak: whence art thou, and what is thy name?'

"Upon this she shook him, but he only snorted and turned round without opening his eyes.

"He said 'Hak,' quoth she, shaking him again; and he snorted again as before.

"'Hak Hak!' cried the woman, laughing. 'Now it is evident this child is abandoned on account of his hump. I will adopt him, even for the drollery of his name!' So she wrapped him in her melaya, and throwing him over her shoulder, carried him home on her back.

"When she reached her house, and had set her burden down upon the floor, she was surprised to see that the little Hak Hak could already walk; and she led him about from door to door, saying to her gossips:—

"'See the beautiful baby I have found under the palm-tree at the corner of neighbour Seid's plot.'

"All the women pronounced him a monster of ugliness, and advised her to carry him asleep to the next village and leave him at the door of the Sheikh's house; but Hak Hak, who was older than he seemed, clung to the skirts of his adopted mother, and made horrible faces at the advisers. The upshot was, that he remained in the village, and grew up towards manhood, much detested by all on account of the mischievous disposition he sometimes manifested.

"Hak Hak was always a lad of ambition; and used to show this feeling very much out of place. One day the Sheikh-el-Beled exchanged a little sheep he had, with half a tail, for a very fine one belonging to the adopted mother of the boy, who upon this reviled him, and said that when he was Sheikh he would exact a buffalo for each leg, an ass for each ear, a goat for each eye, and a sheep for each tooth of the stolen animal.

" 'What!' exclaimed the Sheikh, 'hast thou cast an evil eye upon me? Dost thou envy my post?'

" So he beat him, and sent him away covered with bruises; but Hak Hak muttered as he went along, that when his turn came he would give fifty blows for every blow.

" A little time after this, Hak Hak, who thought himself endowed by nature with the capacity of a merchant, resolved to go to Cairo and seek his fortune. He took two dozen fowls in a kafass, went down to the river, begged a passage on board a boat, and reached the great city in safety."

[Here, be it observed, there was a movement of marked attention in the auditory, who expected the Caireens to be severely criticised; but they were disappointed.]

"When Hak Hak got into the first street, he began by running against a camel-load of wood, and nearly blinding himself; then he tumbled into a shop; and afterwards he got beaten for entangling himself with a harim. On these three occasions he was called a pig, a dog, and a Jew; but the people who abused him soon found that they were not his match in this respect, for he swore with more elegance and point than any Ulema.

"At length, when his body was black and blue, and his throat hoarse, he thought it time to begin selling, especially as his fowls were half dead with hunger and thirst. So he sat himself down at a large gateway and said,—

"'Thus my wisdom suggesteth. This is a large house, and in a large house much is eaten. The cook will presently go forth to market. I will offer my fowls, and she will buy them; and the first stone of my fortune will be laid.'

"Presently a woman came forth; and he addressed her, stating his case eloquently, and explaining all his anticipations; for he thought to charm her by the volubility of his tongue and the beauty of his language."

[Here the Tantawi, who himself had a detestable accent, mimicked the still worse pronunciation of Kafr Hemmir, to the supreme enjoyment of his hearers.]

"When Hak Hak had stated his case, the woman said to him—

"'O excellent and vigorous young man, I will buy thy fowls, which will save me the trouble of going to market. Let me take them in, and I will bring thee the money, for I have not enough with me.'

"She immediately took up the kafass, and disappeared, leaving Hak Hak delighted with his dexterity. But the truth was, he had mistaken the gate of a quarter for the gate of a house; and the woman was a cunning thief, who had understood him to be open to deception. She went home to her den, and related the trick she had played to a companion, who said,—

"'Not to be outdone by thee, I will go and rob this fool of his clothes.'

"Thereupon she went round by another way, and came to the place where Hak Hak was waiting for his money, and was beginning to be very impatient. It happened that there was a well close by; and as she pretended to be very old and feeble, she leaned upon the edge as she crawled along. Suddenly she cried out,—

" ' O Muslim! O good people! help! I have dropped my ring into this well.'

" Hak Hak was the only person near; so he went up to her briskly, and said,—

" ' What wilt thou give me if I dive and bring up the ring?'

" ' O my son,' replied she, ' I will give thee a piece of gold.'

" ' It is a munificent reward,' said he; and forthwith stripped and got down into the well, and began to dive. The first time he came up to the surface, blowing very hard—puff! puff!—and crying,—

" ' Oh, old mother, I find only a stone.'

" ' Try again,' cried she, as she gathered together his clothes.

" He obeyed, and came up blowing puff, puff, puff, and gasping, ' I have found an old shoe.' But she had gone; whilst he, thinking she was still waiting, dived a third time and brought up a piece of broken glass.

" He continued in this wise until he was quite tired, when he climbed up and found that the old woman had fled, leaving him naked and dirty as a worm. He was ashamed to go out into the streets in that plight, and began to roar aloud for help. But every time that the people came out of their houses to see what was the matter, he popped in his head, being too modest to show himself.

"At length a man spied him from a window, and coming forth, dragged him from his hiding-place, and took him into his house, and washed him and his hump, and clothed him and fed him, and listened to his story, at which he laughed heartily. When it was concluded he said,—

"'O Hak Hak, a person of thy talent and beauty is misplaced in Cairo. Thou hadst better return to thy village and trade there. I have heard that the people of Kafr Hemmir think that all wisdom consists in a long beard, and that they have not been blessed with many hairs. I will give thee a case of a cosmetic, which will make their beards grow as long as that of the Prophet. This will be a better means of making a fortune than selling fowls and diving into wells.'

"Hak Hak thanked his benefactor, and departing with the case returned to his village, where he announced what he had for sale before the whole assembled population. To his surprise they all burst out laughing, and made fun of him. He returned desponding to his adopted mother's house, and the world was black before his face; but presently the Sheikh sent privately to buy a small packet; and then the barber; and then the tobacco-seller; and then the coffee-house keeper;—all in private. In fact, before the evening, the whole of his merchandise was sold, and every man in Kafr Hemmir went to bed with his chin steeped in the cosmetic, each believing that both his beard and his wisdom would have doubled in length next morning."

I wish I could reproduce the pantomime by which the morning-scene was described; the snorings, the grunts, the yawns, the impatience for the dawn: for it appears all the patients had been ordered to keep their jaws carefully wrapped up until day-light. At length the wished-for moment arrived.

"Then they all up-rose, and hastily taking off the cloths, which had nearly stifled them, found that their beards came off likewise! They clapped their hands to their chins, and felt them to be as smooth as their knees;

they jogged their wives, and were greeted by screams of laughter; they ran out into the streets, and learned the truth, that the whole population had been rendered beardless by the ointment which the Caireen wag had given to Hak Hak. As all were equally unfortunate, all laughed; but they resolved to punish the unlucky hunchback. He was called before the Sheikh, where the elders of the village had assembled; and when he saw the circle of smooth faces, could not help giggling.

" 'He laugheth, because he hath defiled our beards,' exclaimed the conclave. 'It is necessary to put him to death. We are all friends here; let us thrust him into a bag, carry him to the river, and throw him in, so that no more may be heard of him.'

" This idea was unanimously accepted, and Hak Hak, in spite of his struggles, was carried away in a sack, across an ass's back, towards the river. About noon his guards stopped to rest, and lying down, fell asleep, leaving the hunchback still in his sack. Now it happened that an old man, bent nearly two-double, came driving by an immense flock of sheep; and seeing these people asleep, and a sack standing up in the middle, was moved by curiosity to draw near it.

" Hak Hak had managed to open it a little, and to look out with one eye; which observing, the old shepherd marvelled, saying—'A bag with an eye did I never see before.'

" He demanded, in a low voice, what was the meaning of this. The eye became a mouth, and replied,—

" 'I am the unfortunate Hak Hak, whom these people are taking by force to marry the Sultan's daughter.'

" 'What,' said the old man, who had married thirty-three wives in the course of his life, 'and dost thou repine at such good fortune?'

" 'So much that I would give all I possess to find a substitute.'

" 'Would not I do perfectly well?' quoth the shepherd. 'I am not very old; I have two teeth left, and one of my eyes is good enough: but they would not take me in exchange.'

" 'Oh yes, wallah, they would; if you call yourself Hak Hak: it appeareth that the name is fortunate, and I have been chosen only on this account. Untie the bag, and let me out.'

" The shepherd, whose hands trembled from

age and excitement, liberated Hak Hak, made him a present of his flock, and bade him tie the bag very tightly, lest the change should be discovered. The hunchback did as he was desired, and hastened to retire with his sheep. Meanwhile the villagers, waking up, threw their prisoner again upon the ass, and proceeding on their journey, plunged the poor old man into the river, just as he was dreaming with delight of his first interview with the Sultan's daughter, how he would smile and look pleasant, and how she would bid him be of good cheer."

This was thought a particularly amusing incident. There is little respect for human life in the East; and the hunchback was considered to have done a very clever thing. The great point of the joke was, that just as the poor old shepherd opened his mouth to address his imaginary bride it was filled with cold water; and the Tantawi represented with horrible contortions, deemed highly comic, the somewhat tardy disenchantment of the drowning man.

"Next morning, Hak Hak quietly returned to his village with his flock of sheep, to the great surprise and fear of the beardless people. They thought he must have made a complaint against them, and went up to ask his pardon and congratulate him on his escape.

"'Ah, villains! ah, dogs! ah, pigs!' he exclaimed: 'why did you not throw me into the river where the camels were grazing, or the horses, or the buffaloes? I should then have been a rich man.'

"This hint was sufficient; the beardless held a consultation, and it was resolved that every family should put one of its members into a sack, and throw him in, that he might bring up as much wealth as Hak Hak. They started off that very day, and drowned all the fine young men of the village; but waited a whole week without seeing them come back. So they began to be much alarmed, and went to the hunchback to ask his advice.

"'My good friends,' said he, 'you must have thrown them in among the camels, and they want cords to tie them."

"Upon this they spent all their money in buying cords, and cast them into the river; but another week and a month passed, and at last they understood that they had been tricked. So they rose against Hak Hak, determining to put him to death; but he escaped from their hands, and set out a second time for Cairo.

"It came to pass that there reigned at this epoch in Egypt a king named Mohammed, whose life wore on in such happiness that he became tired of it, and felt every hour weigh heavily on his hands. One day, in his gloom, he said to his Wezeer,—

"'O Wezeer, I desire to hear an empty saying (*kilmet farrah*); find me a man who will say an empty saying to me to-morrow, or I will cut off thy head.'

"The Wezeer endeavoured to expostulate, but it was to no purpose; and he went home wondering what folly had seized the king. He passed all that day in his house; and getting up next morning, rode forth on his mule to ponder on what he should do to save his life. Now it happened that on that very morning the hunchback, Hak Hak, arrived in Cairo, and was seen by the Wezeer reposing by the wayside. He was a droll-looking fellow, whom nobody could pass by unnoticed; so the Wezeer thought to himself, 'Perhaps this deformity may be of service to me.' Then he cried aloud,—

" 'O traveller, wilt thou gain a hundred pieces of gold?'

" Hak Hak replied,—

" 'The woman who stole my clothes offered one piece of gold: it is evident, O Greybeard, that thou desirest to steal my skin.' But the Wezeer explained to him, and he was satisfied.

" They went together to the audience-chamber; and the Wezeer, going in, found the king sitting sullenly looking on the ground. He dared not speak, but waited patiently for the decree of fate. Meanwhile Hak Hak hid behind the door, and showing himself now and then, began beckoning to the king; and when he had attracted his attention, made signs that he wanted to speak to him in private. The king was amused by his droll gestures and grimaces, but did not move; upon which Hak Hak threatened him with his fist, and again began beckoning. At last the king Mohammed rose from his divan, and went out followed by the Wezeer. Hak Hak did not wait, but walked before, still making signs with his hand, shaking his head, and rolling his eyes, and walking with long strides on tiptoe, and wagging his hump from side to side. Thus they proceeded, until they came to the centre of the Kara Meydan, when Hak Hak stopped, and beckoned to King Mohammed to stoop down, that he might whisper in his ear. The king at first was afraid, lest he might bite him; but at last complied, whereupon the hunchback said in a husky voice,—

" 'O king, hast thou ever been to Damascus?'

" 'No,' was the reply.

" 'No more have I, O king,' quoth Hak Hak.

" For a moment the royal one looked puzzled, and then exclaimed,—

" 'Seize this insolent monster, and put him to death.'

" But the Wezeer interfered, and explained that this was the empty saying he had wished to hear; whereupon the king laughed till they were obliged to support him lest he should fall in the dust, and he ordered Hak Hak to relate his history; and when he had heard it, he first caused him to be scourged, and then appointed him Sheikh of Kafr Hemmir. So the hunchback returned to his village, and tormented his enemies; but at last he became a mild man, and was beloved instead of being hated."

This pastoral story of the Tantawi, though

mixed with too much of town life, I considered valuable at the time, as evincing by its composition the state of intelligence among the fellâhs; but from certain hints in it I did not despair of finding more agreeable specimens amongst the unrecorded literature of this neglected race.

CHAPTER XV.

Orientals delight in Filth — A Hidden Jewel — Story of the Early Betrothed — Anecdote of the Braggart — The Drunken Arnaout — Shurdum Burdum — Cause of Gallic Revolutions.

THE story told by the Tantawi did not, as I have said, satisfy me. I felt that there ought to be some other kind of narrative current among the fellâhs, — something still more peculiar to themselves, and painting more exclusively their own manners and ideas. Many specimens subsequently came to my knowledge; but, unhappily, whilst filled with admirable touches, the chief incidents on which they hinged were so gross and indelicate, that it is impossible to give even an account of them. The great mental disease of the Orientals is their love of filth; nor can it be said in their defence that they err from a kind of naïve simplicity. The filth they delight in consists not so much in brutal frankness of language as in odiously ingenious combinations of corrupt ideas. In listening to them, however, it is impossible not to smile at the grotesque humour of their conceptions and the wonderful vivacity with which they body them forth.

In raking amidst these abominations I discovered some pearls, of small intrinsic value, it is true, but of surprising purity. I cannot convey to the reader my delight, because it was principally created by the power of contrast. It was like the breath of spring miraculously breathing through an ice-bound midwinter's day, or like a diamond-sparkling fountain bubbling up at the way-worn feet of a desert-traveller; or like a green island rising over the dipping prow of a vessel that has lost its reckoning in a storm. One especially charmed me by the very simplicity of its construction, the smooth flow of its narrative, the anticipated cheerfulness of its conclusion. It was composed of a series of pictures, almost as innocent as those which tell the fortunes of good boys and good girls to the unqualified satisfaction of the public opinion of our nurseries. Perhaps those who have listened with some displeasure to the equivocal adventures of Hak Hak may be not unwilling to turn for a few minutes to the quiet little chronicle of the Early Betrothed.

In the village of Sheikh Abâdeh, in Upper Egypt, there once dwelt a wise and excellent man, named Ibrahim, who had a young wife, whom he loved as the gardener loves the only rose in his garden. Though the produce of his field was small, and the hand of power weighed heavily on him, he contrived that Ayshë should always have a veil unrent, a pair of trowsers of Frank muslin, and a good melayah, or mantle, from Negadeh.

In the intervals of his field-labour he went among the mounds of the ancient city, and dug up copper coins of the age of Iskender, and odd little images, and bits of gilded glass, which he sold to the strangers who come every year to visit the tombs of their forefathers, and to mourn over the loss of the country that the Muslims have taken from them.

His hut was built near the outskirts of the village, on the margin of the river, just opposite the bank where the wild geese, and the ducks, and the pelicans settle in their season, and where the crocodiles sleep till the going down of the sun. A palm-tree rose up to the sky on one side; and a great sycamore, like a mountain of leaves, stood on the other. In summer time, when the Nile swelled, the inhabitants of the hut could sit on its threshold and bathe their feet without stirring a step; but in spring, Ayshë was compelled to carry her water-pitcher on her head a good distance every morning. On these occasions, the boatmen as they passed would compliment her, and sing songs to her; for they had heard the reputation of her beauty. But she heeded not the praises of any but Ibrahim; and there was nothing wanting to their happiness but one thing, which God had denied, and that was a child, to give them the promise of comfort in their old age.

There were many people in the village willing to bestow the alms of their wisdom upon Ibrahim; and whenever he had his head shaved and his beard trimmed, the barber used to tell him that the sages, and the capable ones, and the learned, were of opinion that, since his wife bore him no child, he should divorce her, and take another. But Ibrahim would devoutly reply, that if the Lord had decreed that he was to be a father, it would come to pass; but that he would not divorce Ayshë, neither separate himself from the partner of his bosom.

They would often talk together of that which was denied them, and Ayshë would abase herself as unworthy of her lord Ibrahim; but he would console her, pressing her to his breast, and kissing her cheek, where the roses bloomed for him alone, and her eyes that spoke with an eloquence refused to her trembling lips. Yet was he troubled in his own mind, and longed anxiously for a son. One night it happened that he was compelled to work late at his shadoof to raise water. It was very dark, and the hour was very tranquil, no sound being heard save the occasional scream of the owl, the mighty flow of the river, and the songs of the other villagers similarly engaged at various distances along the banks. Ibrahim had no heart to sing, for he was thinking of his childless position and repining over his disappointment. He was roused from his reflections soon after the rising moon had flung its dull yellow light over the swelling desert to the east, by observing a number of persons approaching. These were the women of the village, each carrying a supper of boiled lentils and bread for the labourers.

Ayshë separated herself from the group, and came and sat down by the side of her husband.

"Rest awhile and eat," said she, placing the dish, covered with a clean napkin, on the soft grass.

"My heart!" replied he, "I have no courage to eat; for my mind dwelleth on the child which we have not."

Then they fell to talking of their misfortune; and at last Ayshë declared that she would make a pilgrimage to the tomb of Sheikh Seid, who was reputed to relieve married women from the contempt of the world and the derision of their gossips. Ibrahim joyfully consented, and embraced his wife with a heart full of gratitude, and forgot for a while that his shadoof stood still as he sported with her. When she went away she heard his voice burst forth through the night in song, and tremble afar across the country; whilst his companions, cheered by his hearty accents, took up the chorus, and working with redoubled vigour, sent the water dashing beneath the moonlight over the fields in a thousand little channels, like so many arrows of silver.

Ayshë made her preparations next morning, and having embraced her husband, started on the pious pilgrimage, which gave her the privilege of travelling. She walked for many hours, until her little bare feet were sore, and then sat down under some mimosas to rest. The fields and paths were full of people, and there was no danger of her being insulted. She continued her journey until the evening, when she reached her native village, where her mother still lived. Having passed the night, she set forth again alone very early; for she wished to return before evening. But she had now come to a rocky region, and advanced but slowly. All around was desolate, and for a great distance she encountered not a soul. This solitude began to frighten her; and several times, before entering a gloomy ravine, she paused and looked back, as if meditating a retreat without accomplishing the object of her journey. But she remembered the anxiety of Ibrahim, and, her resolution returning, proceeded on her way, though faint and weary, towards the gloomy mountains in which the tomb of Sheikh Seid is found.

The courageous young woman had never been that way before; but her mother, who had performed the pilgrimage for her sake successfully, had exactly described the road; and, moreover, it is believed that whoever sets out in faith to find the tomb, never fails to reach it without guide. Noonday had already arrived, and Ayshë, who had brought no water with her, each time that she attained the summit of a pass cast a longing glance towards the great Nile, which wound afar off in the plain. But it was impossible to turn aside to satisfy her thirst without sacrificing another day; and she was eager to arrive at her destination.

At length she came to a black and gloomy gorge, winding down to a valley surrounded with rocks. Two or three trees rose in the centre, and she remembered that her mother had spoken of a fountain on the road. So she hastened down, picking her way as well as she could amongst the loose stones with her bleeding feet; and soon reached the margin of a pool of clear water, in which two tall palms were waving, as in another sky, and a mimosa, alive with the cooing of invisible doves, doubled its ten thousand leaves. Ayshë was about to stoop down to drink, when a hoarse voice said,—

"Welcome, O sister!"

She looked around and beheld an Arnaout soldier lying under the trees, and gazing with admiration on her face, for she had laid aside her veil in those burning solitudes.

The first impulse of the young pilgrim was to turn and fly; but, reflecting that this would be in vain, she answered the salute with a "Peace be with you," and drank with an appearance of tranquillity. Then she would have departed; but the Arnaout came to her, laughing and rolling his eyes. He was like a hyæna about to spring upon an innocent gazelle. Ayshë did not wait for his approach, but ran back by the way she had come. And well was it that she did so; for, just as the soldier was about to overtake her, a tall woman, armed with a stick longer than herself, appeared and placed herself between them.

"Man," said she, in a grave voice, "is this woman thy wife or thy daughter, that thou pursuest her? If neither, know that I am of the Arabs, and both able and willing to protect the feeble."

To this the soldier replied nothing, but bent his head and went his way; whilst the tall woman, taking Ayshë by the hand, led her back to the fountain, where they sat down and told their respective stories.

The stranger, whose name was Azhara, belonged to a village of Bedawins settled not far from Sheikh Abâdeh; and she also was on her way to the tomb of Sheikh Seid, to obtain the blessing of a child. She was of the tallest of the daughters of Eve; beautiful, but with the strength and vigour of a man. Her arms, though exquisite in form, were capable of lifting a young camel; and many of the robustest youths of her tribe could scarcely wield the staff which she carried about for her protection. On hearing that the little Ayshë, too, was ambitious of being a mother, she smiled and patted her head, and said,—

"Poor child! bring forth a daughter like thyself, and if I am blessed with a son we will marry them together."

Ayshë replied that so it should be, unless Ibrahim otherwise decreed; and after they had rested a little while, they continued their journey.

The road was very difficult, and sometimes the young fellâha found it impossible to climb the rocks. But the Bedawin woman took her up in her arms, caressing her, and saying, "Thou art very helpless to desire to be a mother;" and carried her like a child. Thus they proceeded until they came to the summit of a desert mountain, from which they could look down upon the land of Egypt with its two level plains divided by a river covered with white sails. An immense number of large white birds flew round them as they reached the summit. Their office is to go down to the river and collect the bread-offerings of the passing boats; and to fly over the whole country to bring provisions for the invisible Sheikh, who still lives after death in some unknown cave. The two women brake in pieces the loaves they had brought for the purpose; and the birds, each taking a morsel in its bill, flew away, leaving them to proceed in quiet to the small tomb that stands in the centre of the table land. Here they deposited other offerings, and performed their prayers, invoking the assistance of the Sheikh; and this done, returned by the way they had come.

Both women were perfectly confident of the success of their expedition, and joyfully descended the mountain. But Azhara, over whom fatigue had no power, soon saw that Ayshë was exhausted. The sun had set when they reached the fountain; and darkness quickly gathered in the hollow valley. So Azhara proposed that they should remain there for the night, and taking off her mantle, wrapped her tender companion in it, and bade her sleep as a mother would her baby. For herself she resolved to watch, lest wild beasts might come down to drink at the pool; and she remained the whole night sitting erect and motionless, except when she turned aside to raise the corner of her mantle and gaze at the face of the sleeping Ayshë.

Next morning they continued their journey slowly; for Ayshë felt overcome by a strange weakness. They came upon a herd of camels; and Azhara caught a she-one that was followed by its colt, milked it, and gave her companion to drink. Towards evening only they reached the village where dwelt Ayshë's mother; and here the Bedawin woman kissed the hands of the fellâha, and reminding her of the betrothal of their children, proceeded singly on her way, with her long staff, impatient to rejoin her husband and her tribe. Ayshë, though trembling with something that resembled fatigue, waited until she could no longer see the tall form of the Bedawin woman, nor hear her voice; and then, turning aside to her mother's house, rested there that night, and the next day, and the next night, and afterwards returned to Ibrahim, who waited for her with anxiety. She related her adventures, and it was agreed between them that what Azhara had proposed should be fulfilled.

In due time Ayshë brought forth a daughter, whom she called Lulu; and never did mother more delight in the first offspring of her bosom. The mysteries of maternity amazed and charmed her. Her chief happiness was in beholding her infant feeding upon her breast, and if she had felt her very soul passing away, she would have let it pass rather than disturb those rosy lips. Ibrahim, when work was over, would sit under the sycamore-tree, with his pipe, gazing at this lovely group on his threshold; and though the vivid glances of his young wife were not turned towards him, they made his heart to glow, for they fell with passionate admiration on the round rosy cheek of his only child.

Two years passed before they had any news of Azhara. The fellâh rarely travels beyond his own district. One day, however, Ayshë was down by the water's edge with her pitcher, which she delayed to fill, because she was occupied in gazing at her child, who, just able to stand, was watching, with laughing mouth and eyes, a brood of young geese that were paddling under convoy of the old ones near the bank. Suddenly a voice said, "Salutation, O sister!" and looking up, Ayshë beheld Azhara, with her tall staff in one hand, and leading with the other a little boy, who walked already with a firm step, and glanced seriously from his mother's face to that of the fellâha, as if to know whether this was the friend of whom she had spoken.

The two women sat down, and comparing notes, found that they had become mothers on the same day. Each, after her fashion, was delighted with her progeny; and they took care to renew the betrothal originally proposed by Azhara. But Ayshë was somewhat sad; for she looked forward to the time when her child would quit her to join the tribe of her husband. The Bedawin woman understood her thoughts, and spoke many wise and cheering words — such as her people are familiar with; so that Ayshë was filled with joy, and talked of leaving the village with Ibrahim, to follow her daughter, and many other improbable things: for hope does what it will with the time to come, and knowing not what is written, writes a book of destiny for itself in letters of gold.

Azhara remained a whole month in the house of Ibrahim; and Ayshë, who, in spite of herself, had at first looked with some coldness on Ali, because he always talked of "his Lulu," learned to love the boy, and to regret the time of his departure: so that when Azhara rose one morning, and taking her staff, and kissing the hands of her hosts, went away with her child upon her shoulder, it appeared as if the sun had been removed from the firmament. Ayshë, however, had promised, when a year had passed, to return the visit, and looked forward to the epoch with impatience. Accordingly, one day she started for the Bedawin village, endeavouring to carry her Lulu the better part of the way; but her courage was greater than her strength, and she was obliged to rest at short intervals. Before she had performed half her journey, she began to despair, and sat down by the path-side to weep. But soon Azhara, who had counted the days and hours, appeared coming to meet her; and taking the child on her vast shoulders, preceded the feeble fellâha as lightly as an unburdened camel. On reaching the village, partly formed of houses, partly of tents, she put Ayshë under the care of her husband's mother, and then went about showing to all the women the betrothed of her son. They all blessed the child, and predicted good fortune to it; but they wondered at the beauty and delicacy of Ayshë; and some of them, who had never been at Sheikh Abâdeh, thought that she must be the wife of the Sheikh-el-Beled.

The two families continued in this wise exchanging visits for the space of twelve years, by which time Lulu had grown to be a beautiful girl, distinguished amongst all the children of her age. Now it happened that the fame of her loveliness spread through all the country round; and a wealthy man in a neighbouring village determined to have her for his wife. So he came and demanded her in marriage, quite certain that they could not refuse his presents, among which were a cow and two asses, besides fifty pieces of gold. But they told him she was already betrothed; and he went away with bitterness in his heart.

A long time afterwards there came an order that a bridge should be built over the canal, and this man was appointed overseer over the whole district. He remembered the refusal of his offer; and resolving to revenge himself, ordered that Lulu should be taken among the children employed to carry the earth, and stones, and mortar. It was useless to resist; so, with a great many other boys and girls, the poor child went away at sunrise every morning to work; and blows and stripes were the only salary she received. Workshe, and the other mothers, carried them food during the day; but often the headman drove them back, saying that they interfered with the work. This continued a week, at the end of which a tall, strong lad, came and offered to replace Lulu. The headman wondered at this, and not knowing the meaning of the orders he had received, accepted gladly, saying that the lad was worth five girls. So Lulu returned to her parents, and told them that Ali the son of Azhara had taken her place, and had engaged to work in her stead; at which, like the headman, they marvelled, for the sons of the Bedawins love not to labour with their hands.

When the great man, the overseer, heard what had taken place, he was very angry, and talked of taking back Lulu by force; but one or two just people interfered with their advice, and he refrained. However, he gave orders that Ali should be strictly treated, and beaten if necessary; and, accordingly, he was beaten immediately. The first time he was so astonished that he submitted, looking upon the matter rather as a joke; but the second time he took the headman by the throat, and having inherited the strength of his mother, nearly throttled him: after which, by the advice of his young companions, who knew what would otherwise occur, he took to flight. When the overseer heard this he was rejoiced, and gave orders that Lulu should be again seized; but when they went to fetch her, they found that she was gone, and both father and mother declared they knew not what had become of her. The truth, however, was, that Azhara had come and offered to take the two children together to the settlement of the tribe; and the parents had consented with joy, for they now saw that the overseer was an implacable enemy.

The Bedawin mother reached her home in safety, but scarcely had she arrived when a body of horsemen was seen approaching in the distance. It was guessed that they were come to arrest Ali; and the two children, therefore, were sent into the mountains for concealment. The company of Arnaouts arrived, demanding, with great insolence, that the young fugitives should be given up; but the members of the tribe pleaded ignorance, and soon showed the new-comers that their absence would be preferred. As the sons of the desert, even when settled, are sometimes apt to be irritated by light treatment, the Arnaouts, after talking big a little while, got upon their horses and rode away, declaring that if they caught Ali they would whip him with thorns all the way to Sheikh Abâdeh.

"And I," said Azhara, "will whip the whippers."

They curled their beards at sight of the giant woman, but did not answer.

Ali meanwhile led Lulu rapidly by a narrow defile to a cavern, of which his people only knew the secret. It was an ancient palace of the Kafrs, hewn out of the rock, and was capable of concealing a thousand men from a prolonged search. Here he placed his betrothed in safety, even from a far more active pursuit than he anticipated; and was delighted to have this opportunity of communing with her alone. He was already a man in stature and intelligence, but remained a child in rectitude of heart. So he spoke to Lulu of their betrothal, and of the love he had entertained for her since they first played together, and asked her whether she repined at the contract that had been entered into between their mothers. Lulu, who scarcely yet understood what he meant, soon contrived to let him know that she was willing to abide by the decision of her seniors; and they passed some hours deliciously talking together, until Azhara arrived to announce that they could safely return to the village.

With the exception of a few too naïve expressions suppressed, and certain Oriental ideas abridged or paraphrased, as the case seemed to require, I have pretty exactly followed the original narrative, as given by a man who once begged a passage on board our boat between Minieh and Benisouef. Here, however, it is necessary to retrench, because the commencement of a new cycle of adventures of the heroic character was introduced before the termination of the simple story of the Early Betrothed. This story, indeed, seemed but a kind of pleasant prelude to the narration of a series of incomparably gallant and chivalrous feats which the young Ali performed during his long career; and probably was a recent ornament added to an old legend. For my part, as soon as Ibrahim and Ayshë (evidently nearly our contemporaries, by their manners and the circumstances by which they were surrounded), had been comfortably transferred to the Bedawin encampment, and poetical justice had been satisfied by the punishment of the overseer; and, above all, as soon as Lulu and Ali were married, I ceased to feel much interest in an interminable recital of forays, more or less successful, of interviews with celebrated chieftains, and of episodes, all chaste, it is true, but carrying one into the frigid society of perfect sons of kings, peerless princesses, &c.; — when, I say, the little fellâh drama was terminated, I gradually discontinued my attendance on the recitations. I was satisfied to know that Ibrahim and Ayshë lived in happiness to a good old age; that the tall and stout-hearted Azhara was equally fortunate; and that they were gradually surrounded, without the interference of Sheikh Seid, by a perfect swarm of little grandchildren. The remainder I abandoned to the admiration of the boatmen.

It is worth observing, in illustration of the above story, that it is not uncommon for Bedawins to seek in marriage the prolific daughters of the fellâhs; but that it is extremely rare for them to allow a stranger to take a wife from their tribe. Many of the Arab tribes settled in Egypt, in spite of the assimilating influence of the climate, preserve, in consequence, a very distinct type of countenance, although in nearly every other respect they may be classed with the fellâhs.

A few anecdotes, as specimens of Arab wit, I will venture to introduce, although, for many reasons, they lose by translation.

I.

There was once a man who became the terror of his village by the loudness of his talk and the fierceness of his gestures. He used to carry a naboot a cubit taller than himself; and if anybody attempted to oppose his will, would snort and puff out his cheeks, and bellow like a buffalo. He had a wife, young and beautiful, with gazelle eyes and pomegranate bosom; and altogether, said the poetical narrator (a stolid-looking fellâh) a moony face and a palm stature; but still he ill-treated her until she came to hate him. So she chose a lover from among the young men of the village, and revealed to him the secret that her husband was really a coward; and they agreed together how they should compel him to a divorce. The braggart started on a journey with his wife, who rode upon a donkey. They proceeded together until they came to a melon-field in a lonely place, when the woman said,—

"O my eye, I feel a longing for a melon; but there is no one here who has the courage to steal one."

"Look round," quoth the man, "lest there be somebody coming. I am not afraid, but this is an improper action."

"There is not a goat in sight," replied she.

So he went into the field, carefully peeping to the right and left, and cut the best melon. At that moment the lover appeared with a gun, and exclaimed,—

"O thief!"

The braggart at once fell upon his knees and said,—

"Are there no means of pardon?"

"None," was the reply, "unless thou causest the melon which thou hast cut to grow again."

"That is impossible; but I will ransom myself."

The young man declined to accept anything but the wife; and accordingly the braggart, having pronounced the triple sentence of divorce, went away saying,—

"If that be all, take her; but hadst thou asked to pull my beard, I would have become fierce and killed thee!"

II.

An Arnaout soldier entered a coffee-house drunk, with his sword drawn; and seeing an old woman, toothless, half-blind, and with a tuft of beard on her chin, exclaimed,—

"Let this beautiful damsel sing, or I will slay her."

"I am the mother of four men, who are the fathers of fifteen children," replied the frightened dame.

"My eyes! my heart!" quoth the Arnaout, in bad Arabic, "it is necessary that thou charm me with thy beautiful voice. Sing '*Doos, doos,*' or I will make kababs of thee."

The frightened dame accordingly began to yell out the required stanza, whilst the fellâh customers giggled with delight.

"Ah!" said the Arnaout, sagaciously shaking his head, "what a wonderful thing is drunkenness! This charming voice seems to me no better than the creaking of a sakia!"

III.

A fellâh went to Cairo to make some purchases; but fell in with thieves, who robbed him of all he possessed. He passed the night sleeping in a ruined house, and next day debated whether he should return empty-handed or supply the place of money with cunning. A bright idea struck him.

"I will go to a shop," thought he, "make selection of the best merchandise, and pretend to be a stranger not understanding a word of the language of the country. Perhaps Allah will in this way enable me to escape the obligation of payment."

In this pious and dishonest state of mind

our clown repaired to the Goreeyeh, sat down opposite a merchant, took his pipe, and pointed out some silks and shawls.

"Probably your honour is dumb," quoth the Taggar.

"*Shurdum Burdum,*" replied the fellâh.

These words, not being understood, overawed the trader, who forthwith spread out his best merchandise. After a reasonable repetition of the magical words "shurdum burdum," a selection was made and payment expected. But the roguish customer, quietly taking up the parcel, walked off, and escaped amidst the crowd.

A little while afterwards, a man somewhat resembling the thief passed, and was seized by the enraged merchant. The fellâh protested his innocence; but the other insisted and handed him over to the police, who carried him to prison. Four or five witnesses were brought, according to this satirical narrative, to swear that they had seen him carry away the goods; and he was condemned to the galleys.

Meanwhile the unlucky man's mother-in-law, who happened to be in Cairo, heard of his mischance, and devised how to liberate him.

She took a dead child, wrapped it up carefully in her mantle, and went to purchase at the shop of the merchant. After a little bargaining she suddenly exclaimed,—

"O lewd fellow! O shame to the merchants! Dost thou take liberties with me?"

"Silence, woman!" said the Taggar, quite frightened for his reputation. "What have I done? Hold thy peace!"

But she only cried the louder; whereupon he laid hands on her, and she, dexterously dropping the little corpse concealed in the corner of her mantle, began yelling,—

"*Aie! Aie!* he has killed my child!"

A crowd at once collected; and the neighbour merchants interfered, saying,—

"This is a scandalous story, and must be hushed up."

The supposed culprit professed innocence, and referred to the woman's age and ugliness; but, for the sake of peace, at length agreed to give a large sum. The offer was accepted; a portion of the money served as a bribe for the liberation of the innocent man; and mother and son returned to their village quite satisfied with the adventure.

IV.

An intelligent Arab, having occasion to travel in France during these latter days of gyration, and hearing much discussion as to why its people can never be satisfied with liberty, which they love, and submit with spaniel docility to despotism, which they detest, very naturally applied his mind to the solution of the problem. The first fruit of his meditations was a similitude. He compared the political evolutions of our neighbours — who, by the way, still consider themselves the first nation on the face of the earth, as skinny Miss Tippet, who came out before the peace, continues to believe herself the belle of the season — to the motions of a pendulum possessed by a devil. Charity, or ignorance, led him to seek the cause elsewhere than in the heart of this singular nation. He knew of a country nearly as corrupt, which had remained in blessed immobility — 't was change only that perplexed him — for thousands of years. The Gallic head, then, he argued, must be out of order — that is, as he expressed it, full of foul wind, inflated, blown up like a balloon which the breezes carry whither they will. Being asked to continue his ingenious speculations, and to seek the origin of this deleterious gas, he meditated for a while, and was suddenly illuminated. "*Wa hak en-Nebbi!*" he cried, "the matter is manifest. The French are a bean-eating nation. They eat beans in their soup, beans in their stews, they even make coffee of beans; and is there anything that generates wind so much as beans?" Like most Orientals, he had a story pat to the purpose. "In ancient times," he said (without making any allusion, I am sure, to the late attempted consecration of the bust of a first magistrate), "one of the Pharaohs, in the plenitude of his pride, desired to be worshipped as a god, and resolved to issue a firmân to that effect. But he had a wise Wezeer named Yusuf, who hummed and ha-ed when the project was submitted to him, and at length declared that the people, although tolerably stupid, were not yet sufficiently ripe for the purpose. 'We must take time,' he said, 'and use cunning and artifice; and I do not despair of making the vile multitude worship not only the king, but the very mule which he rides. Let us issue an edict, enjoining all the fellâhs to plant beans throughout the length and breadth of the land.

In a few years, when they have become used to this windy diet, the fragrant incense of their adoration will rise to thy nostrils, O King; and thou wilt be worshipped as a god!'" The Pharaoh listened to advice; and in due time found it an easy matter to bring crowds of devout idolaters, all driven mad by the mechanical operation of the spirit of beans, to the temples which he erected in his own honour. Is it too late for the French to regenerate themselves by giving up the use of *haricots?*

CHAPTER XVI.

Eastern Opinions of Women—Story of the Green Bird and the Two Destinies.

THE light in which women are regarded in Egypt is a subject fascinating, but difficult to discuss. I had once formed a decided opinion thereon; and could have expressed it in three words, short, unliterary, and shocking to ears polite. But I have repented my too hasty judgment, without having been able conscientiously to substitute a more favourable one. I shall refrain, therefore, from making any positive affirmation.

One thing may be advanced as nearly certain—that there is a great absence of spirituality in every race which has accepted the yoke of Islam. Notions on what are called supernatural subjects are, indeed, common; but everything touched by the Mohammedan mind becomes solid, material, fleshly. The paradise it conceives and pants for is nothing more than an elegant lupanar; and with amusing gravity the true believer maintains that married couples do not meet again in another and a better world —unless the husband specially desire it.

In no Eastern country are the positive joys of the anticipated Garden, as they call their Paradise, desired with a keener relish than in Egypt. The roughest fellâh, in his misery and dirt, looks forward with complacent certainty to being magnified into a giant as tall as the palm-groves of his native land; because he believes, contrary to our philosophical poet, that pangs of pain or pleasure increase in intensity with the volume of the body; and figures himself as surrounded with a bevy of maidens mighty-limbed as he, ready to serve him. Thus transformed, in an atmosphere of musk produced by his own skin —southern nostrils are keenly alive to perfumes —he will lie in huge laziness on softer swards than those of Bar Masr, in cooler groves, by a more melodious river; and ever-renewed material pleasures, kisses unfraught with treachery, draughts of no longer forbidden wine, that will "cheer but not inebriate," heavenly kababs and divine pilaus, the rustling of green silks, the glittering of uncounted precious stones, the songs of harmonious angels, will combine to waft him in a delirium of happiness along the tedious stream of eternity, and make him believe that he is still in time.

It is true that some ascetics, in a state of religious intoxication, talk of purer pleasures, of ineffable joys to be experienced in the presence of the Divine Being; but the majority of Egyptians dream only of sexual intercourse—more or less refined, more or less surrounded with circumstances of splendour. It is evident, therefore, that love, in the form under which they conceive it, is to them the highest emotion of which man is capable; but it is equally evident that they despise, from ignorance or knowledge, the focuses on which they are permitted to concentrate the rays of their passion, and long for objects only to be found in heaven or in the dreams of youth.

Leaving a wide margin for exceptions, the Arabs look upon woman as a crafty, dangerous, but useful sex. Like the old philosopher, they say it is impossible to live happily with them, but equally impossible to live at all without them. *Malum necessarium* is a definition that would satisfy the least caustic. Indeed, all the sage witticisms in which libertines are wont to indulge are current in Egypt; and half the stories they love to relate are contrived as illustrations of the cunning and wickedness of the female race.

The following romance, which was related to me several times in various forms, and often with incidents totally different, embodies a good many of the opinions and prejudices of the Easterns on the subject of women. I may here remark that narratives of this kind, either entire or in fragments, form part of the conversation of Orientals, and do not necessarily belong to the repertory of coffee-house story-tellers. It will be observed that the names, characters, and manners are Egyptian, and that the great city of Karamun is merely Cairo concealed under a pseudonyme.

Story of the Green Bird and the Two Destinies.

In a distant country once dwelt a man named Daood, who gained his living by selling firewood. He had a wife and two children, boys; and found it very difficult to earn sufficient to clothe and feed them. For himself he went about nearly naked, like a wild beast, and was apparently so stupified by hard labour and little food that the neighbours called him an idiot, and respected him.

He used to go with a little ragged ass far away into the mountains, where, at the bottom of steep valleys which no one, perhaps, visited but he, grew trees and bushes fed by the dews of night. These he cut and left to dry until his next visit. Sometimes he passed several days, sleeping amidst the rocks; and the wolves and hyænas feared him, for he was fierce and savage as they.

When he returned to the city and had sold his wood, he went home with the produce and gave it to his wife to spend. Then he would sit down and gaze at and admire his two sons, Hassan and Ali, and say, "Allah! is it possible that these two young princes are the fruit of my loins?" For they were lovely as the children of Paradise, and by his side looked like green sprouts springing from the trunk of a withered sycamore.

They were ambitious and proud withal, not associating with children of their own age and loving to walk hand-in-hand through the city; Ali, the younger, to admire the palaces and the guards, and the state of the governor, and Hassan to peep into the shops and warehouses of the merchants.

One day as Daood entered the city gates, he heard the voice of a crier proclaiming an imperative ordinance, and it was this—that on pain of death no private individual was permitted to sell wood by retail, the governor having established a monopoly. Daood began to beat his breast and to tear the little clothing he had left; and having cursed himself aloud, and the powerful in secret, felt more resigned, and went sadly to the public warehouse to dispose of his ass-load of fagots. But there, instead of money, he received a bit of paper, on which was written something he could not read. It was an order on the treasury payable in two years, with which, dismal in countenance, he reached his home, and related to his wife what had happened. The good woman, as women sometimes will when men fear to speak, loudly denounced the tyrant, and in her anger tore the paper to pieces. Then the whole family sat down to a mess of boiled beans, which they salted with their tears.

Daood did not return to the mountains for some days, but sat crouched in a corner of his hut whimpering and bemoaning his fate; but at length his wife said to him,—

"Up, my lord; the neighbours will no longer lend anything, and it is necessary that thou earn money that we may eat and not starve. Go forth with thy ass and bring wood, of which I will keep back part to sell in secret."

Daood saw that there was wisdom in this speech, and took his hatchet and mounted his ass and departed. But when he came to the valley where he had left a provision, he found that fire had fallen from heaven and devoured it. So he pushed further into the interior to cut fresh wood, but wandered long without finding aught but rocks and sand. At length he sat down in despair, and bemoaned his sad fate. Whilst he sat he observed a little green bird crouched in a hollow, as if covering an egg; he watched it silently for some time, remembering that within such birds God's martyrs dwell in Paradise, and found pleasure in the sight. Suddenly the poor thing began to flutter its wings, and curl up its neck, and show all the signs of agitation; and lo! above it was a hawk poising itself, as if about to pounce down, and its bright wicked eyes and crooked claws were visible to Daood. The poor man taking pity on the little green bird, seized a stone and launched it at the hawk, which was frightened, and circling up soon became a spot in the heavens. Meanwhile the green bird had darted like an arrow along the ground, and had disappeared; but Daood, who had kept his eyes fixed on the place where it had sat, saw something brilliant there, and advancing, found it to be a diamond, shaped like an egg and shining like a star. The wood-seeker knew not its value, but said, "This is a pretty thing. I will take it home to the children. It is now too late to seek for more bushes." So he crossed his little ass, and climbed up towards the clouds and down into deep gulleys, and up again, until the green plain was visible and he arrived at the gates of the city.

As he entered, walking beside his weary beast, he kept tossing the diamond in his hand.

Now a Jew who was passing along saw and coveted it, and said to him,—

"O Sheikh, wilt thou sell me that piece of stone for ten pieces of gold?"

The wood-cutter thought he was laughing at him, and replied,—

"Not for a hundred."

"Let it be a hundred," whispered the Jew, pulling him by his ragged sleeve into a by-place.

"A thousand," said the cunning fellâh, guessing the truth.

Whereupon the Jew, having sworn by Father Abraham that it was too much, counted a thousand pieces of gold, and begged that he might have the first offer of any other such jewel that might be found.

The change thus wrought in the position of Daood was great. Some go so far as to say that he returned every morning to the mountain and procured a fresh egg. At any rate he became a wealthy man, built a magnificent house, and was envied and respected by his neighbours. Wealth provokes envy, but it buys respect; and the world prefers being trampled on by a golden hoof to feeding the horse that neighs for its provender. How the journeys to the desert came to cease I do not remember, but at length the green bird was captive in the house of Daood, who had only to put his hand into the cage whenever he wished to obtain an egg—always sold to the same Jew for a thousand pieces of gold.

The fortunate wood-cutter remained a quiet simple man, devoting himself principally to attending on his beautiful friend and benefactor, which he tamed and taught to sit on his finger, and entirely reconciled to its captivity. Indeed, says the narrator, it would have been a very foolish bird to have preferred flying about the wild desert, in danger from hawks and snakes, to living in a golden cage, with delicate food at command, and tended as if it had been a son of Adam. But after a time the good Daood thought it necessary, in token of gratitude for what he had received, to make a pilgrimage to Mekka. So, leaving his children and his bird to his wife's care, he departed for the holy city.

The story here removes its scene to the heart of the Jew-purchaser of the diamonds. There is no article of Muslim faith more firmly rooted than this, that the Jew is an accursed odious being, with but one passion—the love of gold; and one amusement—the working of evil on true believers. This said Hebrew, therefore, is represented as sitting in an underground cave upon heaps of gold, which he occasionally raked with his crooked fingers, plotting the acquisition of fresh wealth and the ruin of Daood. How he came by the knowledge which guided him is not explained. Are not people of his race in communion with the evil one? However this may be, the Jew knew a thing or two about the green bird; not only all its relations with Daood, but also that its heart and liver were endowed with magical power, so that whoever ate the first would become a king, and whoever ate the second would have unlimited wealth at command. He therefore pondered in his head how he might indulge in these delicate morsels.

Having matured his plan, he went to the palace where resided the wife of Daood, and demanded to be introduced to her presence, that he might pay his respects. The harim opened before him, — it is not explained why; perhaps because the lady was old, perhaps because the narrator, being of humble position, transferred the facility of intercourse he had been accustomed to to the now aristocratic family of the wood-cutter. At any rate, admitted was the Jew; and being of eloquent tongue, he easily succeeded in cajoling the wife of the poor fellâh. In fact, he worked enchantment on her; for she became an automaton in his hands, invited him to supper, and at his suggestion ordered the green bird to be killed. The Jew thought himself sure of success, and waited patiently for the costly meal.

But when the poor bird was killed in the kitchen by the cook, a slave-girl, and placed upon the fire, it diffused a savoury smell; and the children Hassan and Ali came in and asked, as children will, for a taste. The cook would not cut the meat; but gave to the younger the heart, and to the elder the liver. This done, she proceeded with her work, and served hot.

When the Jew saw the bird placed before him, he seized it with avidity, and looked for the expected tit-bits; but he saw them not. His crooked fingers trembled as they tore to pieces the bird; his visage became as yellow as gold; his eye grew round and fierce like those of a rat; the nostrils of his thin nose opened like the gills of fishes; his teeth showed amidst his beard like the fangs of a wild boar. At length he shouted out for the heart and the liver.

"O master!" said the wife of Daood, terrified at his anger, "it is probable that the cook has laid them aside. Let her be called."

The slave-girl came, and told the truth; whereupon our Jew insisted that the children should be killed, that he might eat them. The mother, under the influence of fascination, consented; and cookey received orders to commit the double murder: but, instead of obeying, she caused the children to fly. Whereupon the Jew returned to his gold-cellar, and was found, some days afterwards, lying dead with rage upon a heap of leaves, into which his accursed wealth had been changed by divine wrath.

CHAPTER XVII.

Sequel of the Story of the Green Bird and the Two Destinies.

So far we have a good nursery tale, in which the incidents are fancifully contrived in order to cast out upon the world two lads, each with the seal of good luck upon him. In their hurried flight they separated; and the story follows the fortunes of the elder, Hassan. After a variety of adventures, he arrived one evening at a great city named Karamun, very poor, and tired, and miserable. All that he possessed were a pair of saddle-bags and a mule, which, with cool disregard of the rights of property, he had stolen from where he found them, under a tree. Before entering the city, with the prudence of a Don Rafael he filled the bags with stones, that he might appear to possess some wealth, and boldly rode through the gates, where custom-house officers were probably not yet stationed.

It happened that evening that a Kunafiyeh, or seller of sweetmeats, was disputing with his wife which was the right side of a melon. They sat opposite each other, with the fruit between them; and the man said: "This is the right side, because the other is the left;" but the woman replied: "Not so, son of a dog! dost thou not see that the right side is nearest my right hand?" The dispute grew warm, until at last the woman, who was old and wicked—according to the Arabs, all old and ugly women are especially wicked—began to swear, and to say:

"*Wallah el Azeem!* thou shalt not sleep to-night until this matter is decided between us."

The Kunafiyeh should have given up the point at once; but women have aggravated wiser folks into obstinacy; and he chose a middle course, saying,—

"Let the first stranger who cometh down the street be arbiter betwixt me and thee."

At that instant a comely youth, riding on a mule, approached; and the couple ran out to meet him, and one took the bridle on one side, and the other on the other, both crying,—

"O our lord, judge thou between us."

And they dragged him from the saddle before he could answer, and hustled him into the room where the melon had been; but lo! in the meantime a black slave—(Negroes are as surely thieves as Jews are misers and old women shrews)—had stepped in and carried off the object of dispute. The Kunafiyeh shrugged his shoulders, and said,—

"It is well. Let contention cease."

But the wife stated the case, and insisted on a decision in her favour. Whereupon Hassan, who was wise above his years, hemmed, coughed, and spat, and delivered his opinion:

"It is evident, O mother," quoth he, "that thou knowest all things. There are two sides to a melon, but only one right side; and the left side is opposite to the right side. Now, as the right side was on thy right side, it could not have been on the other side, and this good man will see the reasonableness of thy opinion."

The narrator, whose knowledge of human nature seems to have been extensive, avers that the woman felt tenderly towards her husband as soon as he was presumed to be in the wrong, embraced him, and invited Hassan to stop with them and to spend the night, as he was a stranger.

The youth accepted, nothing loth, and when supper was ready, ate the greater part of the mutton and bamiæ; so that the Kunafiyeh raised his eyebrows, and the woman inwardly repented her hospitality. But both looked at the heavy saddle-bags, and thought: "The stranger is rich, and will reward us." They all lay down to sleep in the same room; and Hassan, being travel-weary, waked not until near the hour of morning prayer. The Kunafiyeh and his wife were talking together in a low, husky voice — he saying that it would be a sin, and she scorning his scruples, and urging that a golden hand could not receive the stain of blood. So Hassan knew that they were plotting his death, and, in spite of the danger, laughed inwardly to think he should be killed for a bag of stones. He opened one eye a little, and saw the man and woman sitting over the saddle-bags, which they had opened. The man's head was turned aside, but he gazed askance at the contents; whilst the woman was dipping in her hand, and raising it a little, so that the pieces of gold ran through her fingers like water through a sieve. Now Hassan being a youth slight of make and feeble of muscle, understood that this miracle which had been performed placed his life in danger, and he closed his eyes, and recommended himself to God. Suddenly there was a scuffle, and starting up, he beheld the Kunafiyeh standing over the dead body of his wife, whom he had slain, that his roof might not be polluted by murder.

The story forgets for a time this tragic incident. Hassan and the Kunafiyeh became at once boon companions. The liver of the green bird continued to work its effect; and the riches of the happy pair were limited only by their desires. Their first care was to build a marble palace, with columns of emerald, and floors of jasper, and marvellous fountains. Of course, the harim was well stocked with beauties, and well guarded by the most ferocious eunuchs. The Kunafiyeh acted as the Wakeel (agent, or major-domo) of his young friend, and exhibited the most wonderful sagacity in the art of spending. Their life was one series of banquettings and revellings; and people gave them the title of The Most Happy.

But satiety, that constant satellite of unbounded wealth, came to interfere with their delight — at least with the delight of Hassan; for the Kunafiyeh had restrained himself in one particular, and had steadily refused all the lovely maidens and tempting hooriyehs which his friend had offered to bestow upon him. "Accursed be women!" was his constant exclamation: "their glances are daggers; the dew of their lips is poison; and the touch of their rosy-tipped fingers is more dangerous than the bite of a serpent." With stoical indifference he went once a-week to the market, and inquired if there was any marvellous beauty to be sold; and in case he was satisfied, upon inspection, with any damsel, he paid her price without bargaining, and added her to his friend's harim. Sometimes Hassan would scarcely notice those additions; he had become so lazy-minded, that he knew not the names of any of his handmaidens.

Upon a certain day the Kunafiyeh went to the market, and was told that Abu Taleb, the principal dealer, had just received from Persia the most perfect damsel of her age. He immediately asked to see her, and being a privileged man, was at once admitted into the apartment of the slave. The cut-and-dry poetical phrases of the East will scarcely convey an idea of the astounding beauty of this maiden. Her eyes were more brilliant than those of a gazelle; her nose was like a pillar of silver; her mouth resembled a rose-bud; her teeth were strings of pearls; her whole face, indeed, was moony; whilst her stature was like that of the palm; her breasts like pomegranates; and, in fine, her hips so heavy that she could scarcely rise from a sitting posture. No wonder that the Kunafiyeh at once fell in love with her, and bought her with Hassan's money, and took her to a house of his own, and made her his concubine. In obedience to a kind of presentiment, he did not mention the circumstance to any one, being determined to enjoy his felicity in secret.

The Kunafiyeh was not remarkable for beauty, or for manners captivating to the softer sex. He was past the meridian of life, mean of aspect, and seemed by nature intended for a buffoon; but of these deficiencies he was not aware, or, at any rate, made no account of them. Was he not lord and master over the beauteous Zeyneb, and as much entitled to enjoy her love as to eat the grapes from the bunch which he had paid for in the market?

Now Zeyneb was of another mind, and sought only for means of liberation from her disagreeable master. One of her servants told her that in truth she had been bought with the money of Effendi Hassan, the wealthiest of the sons of wealth, and the most charming of youths. From mere description she became enamoured of the friend of her master, and longed ardently to see him. The opportunity at length occurred. She went forth one day to visit the shops of the merchants, and sat with Taggar Mohammed buying merchandise to pass her time. A youth mounted upon a mule, with a serving-man on each side to support him, came riding slowly down the bazar, and stopped at the shop of the said Taggar. His servants lifted him from his saddle, placed cushions for him, and lighted his pipe, whilst the merchant stood on his feet, and bowed, and blessed God for the honour of receiving Effendi Hassan. Zeyneb at once understood that fortune had favoured her designs, and gazed amorously on the languid youth, who, partly from indolence, partly from affectation, at first paid no attention to her. When, however, she, as if by accident, dropped her veil, and exhibited the full lustre of her countenance, he started with amazement. The dart of love entered his heart. He forgot all the wondrous beauties of his harim; and all his wealth appeared to him as nothing, if it could not purchase the possession of that peerless damsel. He spoke tenderly to her, but she in her turn pretended not to regard him, and exerted all the arts known to her sex to stimulate his passion. The discreet merchant, in order not to disturb them, affected to talk with a neighbour; and thus, in half an hour, Zeyneb was enabled to acquire complete ascendancy over the youth. At length, in obedience to his impassioned entreaties, she consented to receive him that evening, if he promised to come alone, armed with a sword; and he went away exalted to the seventh heaven of delight. All his languor had disappeared. This adventure dispelled the gloom of satiety; and recalled him to the vigour of youth.

When night came, he left his palace alone, and repaired to an appointed place, where a black slave-girl waited to conduct him to the residence of Zeyneb. He arrived in safety, and was admitted into a large saloon, where his newly-loved lady waited for him with impatience. Nothing, he thought, could now interfere with his happiness; but the wicked damsel had other thoughts in her head besides those of love.

"O my beloved," said she, "I must be all thine or not thine at all. Take thy sword and enter the adjoining chamber, and slay the man that thou beholdest sleeping on the divan."

"Nay, my mistress," responded Hassan, "that will be a heavy crime; and my heart refuses."

At these words fire flashed from her eyes.

"Know, boy," said she, "that if thou doest not my bidding, I will call aloud, and the servants and eunuchs will come, and they will put thee to death. Follow me, therefore."

So she took up a lamp, and preceded Hassan into the adjoining chamber, where the Kunafiyeh lay sleeping, with his face towards the wall. As she moved, she turned a languishing glance towards Hassan, who became intoxicated with passion, and thought: "It is better to kill than to be killed." He raised the sword; but at that moment a fly settled on the cheek of the sleeping man, and caused him to roll round, so that his countenance became visible, and Hassan knew him. The sword descended; but not on the neck of the Kunafiyeh. The head of the treacherous Zeyneb rolled upon the floor.

Then Hassan waked his friend, and told him the story, and the two consulted together how to dispose of the dead body; for the Sultan of Karumun had lately issued an edict, forbidding all private men to slay even their slaves. They agreed to put the trunk into a box, and the head into a basket, and to carry them to the river and cast them in, so that the fishes alone should know the secret. What was said was done, and the Kunafiyeh started by one road with the box, whilst Hassan went by another bearing the basket, which he filled with leaves, and covered with oranges.

Now it happened that the Sultan, Ali Mustafa, was that night parading the streets of his capital, to see that all was quiet. Some of his guards found a man crawling along in the darkness, with a heavy load upon his back, and stopped to question him. He was too much terrified to reply—his face became white, and his teeth chattered. Then one of the soldiers noticed that blood was trickling between the crevices of the box, and smote the Kunafiyeh on the cheek, calling him dog. The officer caused an examination to be made, and found the headless trunk of the murdered Zeyneb.

"This is a serious business," said he, "and must be referred to the Sultan."

When the Sultan and his suite came up, surrounded with torchmen, the case was stated. Upon this, Ali Mustafa, who was young of years, and therefore compassionate, smote his breast, and cried aloud, saying,—

"Am I invested with the sword of justice, and are the daughters of my people thus slain and dismembered in my despite?"

Then the Kunafiyeh took courage from despair, and exclaimed,—

"O king! this woman came righteously by her death; and if thou wilt permit me, I will relate my story, and convince thee of my innocence."

"Speak," replied the Sultan. Whereupon the Kunafiyeh related his own story, and the story of Hassan, even from the beginning. Then the Sultan said,—

"O soldiers, disperse through the city, and seek for a man bearing a basket containing a head, concealed under oranges. When thou hast found him, treat him gently, and bring him before me. As for this Kunafiyeh, imprison him in one of the chambers of my palace; and let the damsel be buried decently."

Meanwhile Hassan had proceeded some distance on his way, and had passed the city gates and reached the country, when he saw torches moving in the distance, and was afraid of pursuit. "It will be better for me," he thought, "to dispose of this head at once; and not to trouble myself to go to the river." So he set the basket down by the roadside, and escaped across the fields, intending to re-enter the city by another way. But when he approached he found the gates closed, and not daring to demand admittance, sought a resting-place for the night among the tombs.

Those who know the mechanism of Eastern romances will not be surprised to learn that a female ginn beheld Hassan as he slept, became enamoured of him, and transported him to a distant country. Escaping from her thraldom, he wandered over the earth, meeting with a variety of surprising adventures, always wealthy, but prevented for a long time from returning to Karamun. His love-passages are, of course, numerous. He has to do with princesses, daughters of wealthy merchants, slaves; but, in every case, he is either betrayed or falls into dire misfortune. At length he finds a perfect beauty and incomparable character in the wise Kadoogah, queen of the Emerald Isles, who marries him against the laws of her country, which condemned her to celibacy. She escapes in his company by the exercise of the magic art, which she had, of course, learned from an old nurse; and they both set out for Karamun.

Meanwhile the Kunafiyeh had been once more in danger of his life. The morning after his arrest, the guards reported that the man with the basket could not be found; and the Sultan began to believe that, in reality, Hassan had been murdered likewise. In his indignation, therefore, he decreed, that if the truth was not made manifest before noon the Kunafiyeh should die. Accident interfered to prevent the execution. Just as it was about to take place, a fellâh, bearing a basket of oranges, passed before the windows of the palace. One of the women bought it, and discovered the head. This proved so far the truth of the story told by the Kunafiyeh, who was not only pardoned and elevated to high rank, but learned to his joy that the Sultan was no other than Ali, the younger son of Daood the woodcutter, who had thus found the benefit of eating the heart of the green bird. In due time Hassan arrived with Queen Kadoogah; and the brothers, having at length sent news of their prosperity to their parents, and caused them to come to Karamun, lived happily together, until they were visited by the destroyer of delights and the divider of companions.

CHAPTER XVIII.

Destruction of Egyptian Monuments—The small Pyramids of Ghizeh—By whom ruined—Arches of Ghizeh—Attempted Demolition of the Pyramid of Mycerinus—Modern Proposition—Care of ancient Monuments by Kings—Use of Antiquities—Popular Opinions—Treasure-seekers—their Ignorance and Cupidity—Accidental Success—Dr. Abbott's Ring—his interesting Museum—Moderation of the Fellâhs—Greediness of Citizens—Treasure-seeker's Guide—Magicians—Charms—Clairvoyance—Ibn Khaldoun—Buried Wealth of ancient Nations—Berber Talbehs—their Tricks—Incitements to Treasure-seeking—Magic—A wonderful Receipt for drying up Water—Artifices of Impostors—Rakiz—Burying Treasure with the Dead—Tax on Treasure-seekers—Fellâh Belief—Antiquarian Mischances—Treasure-Trove.

I HAVE more than once in the course of the foregoing pages alluded to the tremendous progress which the destruction of the monuments of ancient Egypt has made, and is still likely to make. In Lower Egypt, with the exception of an obelisk and a pillar at Alexandria, there is now scarcely anything worth mentioning: the Pyramids are partially protected by their magnitude, but are not exempt from danger; whilst in Upper Egypt it may be said that the continued existence of the most precious relics of antiquity is merely accidental. Two temples, which had never attracted the attention of travellers, have lately been destroyed at Sheikh Fadl; several of the propylæa at Thebes have been toppled down by blasting; and innumerable tombs have been utterly and irremediably ruined.

Nothing gives a grander idea of the architectural achievements of the ancient Egyptians than the labour which, for thousands of years, has been from time to time expended in pulling down what they built up. "Formerly," says an Arab writer of authority, "there existed at Ghizeh a considerable number of small pyramids, which were destroyed in the time of Salah-ed-Deen. Their destruction was the work of Karakoush, a Greek eunuch, one of the emirs of that prince's army, and a man of considerable genius. He was superintendent of the buildings of the capital, and it was he who raised the wall which encircles Fostat, Cairo, and the land that separates those two cities, as well as the citadel built on Mount Mokattam, and the wells that are still seen there. He used the stones that came from the small pyramids in constructing the Arches at Ghizeh—a work worthy of the highest admiration, and comparable with those of the giants. The remains of the pyramids destroyed by Karakoush are still to be seen."

"When Melek Alaziz Othman ben-Yusuf succeeded his father, he suffered himself to be persuaded by certain persons of his court, senseless people, to demolish the great pyramids; and they began by the Red Pyramid, which is the least considerable of the three. The Sultan sent sappers, miners, and quarrymen, under the guidance of some of the principal officers and emirs of his court, with orders to destroy. They accordingly established their camp near the pyramid; and collected from every side an immense number of workmen, whom they entertained at great expense. They remained at their post eight months, occupied with all their followers in carrying out the order given them, removing every day, after great exertion, one or two stones. Some men worked with wedges and levers, others pulled from below with ropes and cables. When one of the stones fell it made a frightful noise, which resounded afar off, shaking the earth and the mountains thereof; and it sunk in the ground so deep that equally great exertions were required to get it out again. Then they broke these blocks to small pieces with wedges, and cast them at the foot of the hill.

"After having thus remained a long time encamped at that place, and exhausted the money placed at their disposal, as well as their strength and courage, they were compelled to abandon the undertaking. They only succeeded in spoiling the look of the pyramid, and demonstrating their own impotence. This happened in 593 (A.D. 1196). When we look at the stones that have been removed, it would seem as if the pyramid must have been destroyed to its foundation; but when we raise our eyes to the monument itself, it still seems almost intact.

"Being one day a witness of the extreme trouble which it cost to drag down a single stone, I spoke to one of the inspectors, and said, 'If you were offered a thousand pieces of gold to replace one of those blocks, and fit it as it was before, do you think you could succeed?' His answer was, that for ten times the sum they could not; and he confirmed what he said by an oath."

In our own days the same idea has been started; and European engineers have offered to do what the bunglers of Melek Alaziz's time abandoned in despair. It has even been proposed to fill the Queen's chamber with gunpowder, and thus blow the whole pile to atoms; but considerations on the proximity of Cairo caused the plan to be rejected with affright. The object of destruction would not now be bigotry or hopes of finding treasure, but simply to obtain food for the lime-kilns.

"In former times," says Abd-el-Latif, "the kings watched with care over the preservation of these precious remains of antiquity; and although declared enemies of the peoples of which the colossal statues were the work, do not allow them to be injured or destroyed for the mere love of mischief. This wise conduct had many reasons. In the first place, they considered these monuments as a species of annals useful to recall the memory of past ages. Secondly, they are, as it were, witnesses that depose to the truth of the revealed books: for such idols and the nations that adored them are mentioned in the Korân;

and the sight of what remains adds the testimony of every man's personal experience to that of authority, and confirms the truth of religion. [This Eastern Protestantism is sensible enough.]

"These monuments also serve as warnings of the future, and call our attention to the destiny reserved to all the things of this world. Besides, they give us a sketch of the history and manners of the ancient nations of the earth; we learn, in studying them, to what degree of advancement in the sciences they had reached, what was the acuteness of their minds, and such-like circumstances. Now, these are matters of which the knowledge satisfies the soul of man.

"But in these days—[the eternal complaint of unphilosophical critics, who place their standard in the past, not in the future]—in these days the reins have been given to men, and nobody has troubled himself to repress their caprices. Every one has been permitted to act as seemed good to him. Abandoned thus to their own fantasies, which have become their only rule of conduct, and knowing no check which could prevent them from acting according to the impulse of their prejudices or their passions, men have yielded to the current of their natural inclinations, obeying all the impressions of their blind caprice and prejudices. When they perceived monuments of colossal grandeur, their aspect inspired them with terror; they framed false and foolish ideas of the nature of these remnants of antiquity; and as their whole thoughts were centered in the sole object of their vows, and the only thing capable of charming their hearts, they felt what a poet has said of a wine-bibber:—

> 'Where'er his eyes their glances turn,
> They see bowls sparkling to the brim.
> The beggar pleads,—'Fill up,' he cries;
> All men are Ganymedes to him!'

"Thus whatever appeared to point out anything at all was to them the sign of a hidden treasure: they could not see an opening in the side of a mountain without believing it to be the road to some wonderful mass of wealth: a colossal statue, in their eyes, was the guardian of money buried at his feet, and the implacable avenger of any attempt against it. They had recourse to all sorts of artifices to destroy and disfigure these statues; mutilating the faces, for example, like people who hoped thus to obtain their ends, and who feared by more vigorous attacks to draw ruin upon themselves. They have split open and bored holes in solid blocks of stone, imagining them to be strong boxes filled with immense sums, — like thieves who enter a house by any way rather than the door, and are ever on the watch to snap at opportunities.

"Among the openings that attract their attention are some in which it is only possible to enter by crawling, or shuffling backwards; whilst in others it is necessary to work face to the ground, and often only the very slimmest person can thus effect an entrance. Many of these openings are merely natural fissures in the mountains, leading to nothing.

"Among the greedy men of whom we speak, some who were well to do in the world have lost all they had in these fruitless researches: others, already poor, go to wealthy men and excite their cupidity and inflame their hopes, as well by profane oaths, as by hints of secrets which they profess to have discovered and be sole possessors of. Thus they cause their victims to lose their money and their reason at the same time; and the unhappy wretches are at length rewarded for their stupid credulity by frightful misery.

"There are certain circumstances which contribute really to strengthen their cupidity and sustain their courage. Now and then they find under earth vast caves solidly built, in which are enclosed immense numbers of corpses, which have been deposited there at very distant periods. These bodies are wrapped in shrouds of canvass; some in as much as a thousand yards of cloth. The Bedawins and Arabs take away these shrouds when they have any solidity, and use them to make garments for themselves, or else sell them to paper-manufacturers, who make thereof paper for the use of grocers."

The worthy Doctor Mowaffik then goes on to say that small quantities of gold, jewels, and precious stones, had been occasionally found. Among other instances, he mentions lingots taken from the mouths of corpses in the cemetery of Abusir, or rather of Sakkarah. Even at present, gold ornaments, rings, and coins are discovered from time to time, and sold to travellers, who, as the fellâhs now know well, give more than the price of the gold. The ring in the possession of Dr. Abbott of Cairo is, perhaps, the most authentic specimen that can be cited, which explains the very large sums that have been offered for it by amateurs.

I may mention, by the way, that the invaluable collection of which this ring forms a part has this summer been sent to America direct. It is a great pity that its owner has not been encouraged at least to show it in England, before shipping it across the Atlantic. No European museum possesses so complete and beautiful a collection of the more fragile spoils of ancient Egyptian civilisation; and had it been exhibited in London, perhaps public opinion might have forced Government to purchase it, instead of wasting money, as was once proposed, in the transference of a huge obelisk to I know not which fashionable square. I like to write on this subject, because Dr. Abbott has on his conscience the destruction of no temple or tomb, in whole or in part. Most of his specimens would by this time have been smashed to atoms, or dispersed over the world (in those private collections which travellers bring home to astonish their friends, and thrifty housewives, hateful of litters, soon stow away in garrets), had not he devoted his time and his money to intercepting them. Most probably Dr. Abbott's museum will be purchased in America; and we may not envy its possession to the future depositories of civilisation. However, I must confess that it would have been pleasant to me to see this singularly rich assortment of curiosities transferred to a place which seems to have been built for the purpose, but to have been long in search of permanent employment—the Egyptian Hall.

To return, however, to the treasure-seekers of Egypt. In spite of the sensible view taken of the subject, some six hundred years ago, by Abd-el-Latif, the people still believe profoundly in the existence of hidden stores of wealth throughout the land. As, however, they also continue to believe that buried money is under the guardianship of supernatural beings, and can only be got at by the aid of powerful talismans, they rarely, in spite of their excessive desire of riches, suffer themselves to be troubled by longings that cannot be accomplished. The marvellous treasures of El-Berqeh remain undisturbed; and at Shabour, the huge stone on which a cock comes out every night from underground to chant, has not been removed, although the wealth of a kingdom is buried beneath.

From time to time, however, bold and impious men, for the most part inhabitants of cities, ruined debauchees, or confirmed sensualists, having sought the assistance of magic, undertake excavations that have, it is said, been frequently crowned with success. The magicians employed on these occasions are generally Maghrebbis, men from the West, from a country where the belief in supernatural agencies is even still more deep-rooted than in Egypt, and which sends forth whole troops of adventurers, who have no other means of living than the arts of magic. The public mind is prepared to entertain them by an immense number of treatises that have been composed on the receipts by which concealed wealth may be discovered. One of these points out in detail all the places of Egypt where researches may profitably be made, and all the means necessary to be adopted. It bears a name that may be translated "The Treasure-seeker's Guide."

I have seen several of these men, who, when they cannot find any one disposed to meddle with the strong boxes of the ginn, are content to make magical computations, to ascertain the whereabouts of a stolen slipper or a stray goat, or to soothe the pangs of love by prophecies or the construction of charms. I bought a slip of paper curiously inscribed, said to have the virtue of constraining the affections of the fair. It cost ten paras, I think, and will probably one day bring me a return of a pennyworth of love. Sitt Madoula professed to have found a lost spoon by the aid of one of these gentlemen — evidently a wise sorcerer; for, after covering a paper with strange figures, he gave his advice thus: — "Search in the room where the spoon was last seen, and if it be not there it is stolen!"

During my last residence in Alexandria I heard several reports of hidden treasures, and was strongly urged to take part in an attack on a very rich *placer*. Being a heretic, I had no fresh danger of eternal fire to incur. Some young Levantines, about the same time, were taken in hand by a circumcised Subtle from Fez, and persuaded to spend a good deal of money in incantations, which were to fill about a hundred jars with gold. Solitude, and drugs, and perfumes, seem to have produced such an effect upon them, that they absolutely imagined they saw the gold pieces brimming over.

Ibn Khaldoun, an old Arab writer, has a curious chapter in his "Historical Prolegomena" in support of the thesis, "that the search for treasures and buried wealth is not a natural means of gaining a livelihood and becoming rich." What appears to us mere trite common sense was in his mouth great wisdom. I extract some of his remarks from De Sacy's translation, because in nearly all their details they would apply exactly to our own days.

"Among the inhabitants of great cities there are found many people of weak mind, who desire with ardour the discovery of treasures buried in the earth, and who found on such discovery their only hope of fortune. These good folks believe that the earth contains all the riches of the ancient nations, confided to the guard, and put under the seal, of certain talismans; and that to destroy the magical charm of these talismans it is necessary first to know them, and then employ such fumigations, conjurations, and sacrifice of victims, as are proper to neutralise their power. Thus, for example, the inhabitants of the principal cities of the province of Africa imagine that the Franks, who reigned there before the Muslims, concealed under the earth their treasures, and have inscribed in certain books notes of these deposits, in order to preserve the knowledge thereof until a favourable opportunity offers of withdrawing them. In the eastern provinces a similar conduct is attributed to the Copts, the Greeks, and the Persians. On this subject many adventures are related, resembling romances. It is said that certain people, in making excavations, have reached places where were deposited treasures, of which the talisman was unknown to them, and have been scared by spectres brandishing naked swords; or else that the earth trembled and threatened to swallow them up. A multitude of such fables are current.

"In the Maghreb are a great number of Talbehs, among the Berbers, who, knowing no trade and having no proper means of gaining a livelihood, make acquaintance with rich persons, and exhibit certain papers covered with barbarous characters or Arabic writing. They pretend them to be the translations they have made of the original records of hidden treasures. By such means they seek to extract something from the persons whom they address, by exciting them to make researches, pretending that they require a patron who will share their profits, and protect them from the punishments and persecutions to which they become liable for such unlawful proceedings. They often perform tricks and pretended incantations, without having any real knowledge of the art of magic. Many weak-minded individuals take the bait, and make excavations at night, in order to escape the attention of the magistrates and the police. When they find nothing, they say that it is because they did not know to what talisman the guardianship of the treasure was confided."

"Among the causes," pursues this philosophical writer, "which incite men to these researches, is the spirit of luxury and a taste for the enjoyments of life pushed to such an excess that ordinary resources cannot suffice. When a mind desirous of pleasure can no longer be satisfied by the legitimate returns of labour, recourse is had to search for some unlimited treasure. The imagination is excited by the idea of acquiring without trouble an immense fund, that will gratify that greedy lust of enjoyment which enslaves those who once yield to it. Thus those who undertake these unlawful researches are generally men accustomed to pleasure and easy life, courtiers and citizens of great cities—as Cairo, for example. Their whole minds are given up to their vain projects, and whenever a caravan arrives they hasten to put questions upon extraordinary facts connected with hidden treasures, being equally fanatical on this subject as on that of alchemy. Thus the inhabitants of Cairo discourse with all the Talbehs of the Maghreb whom they meet, in hopes of gathering some profitable hints. Among their topics of conversation a common one is how the earth may be made to absorb water, because they think that most hidden treasures are buried in the bed of the Nile; and this excuse is one often given by the magicians they employ, when unsuccessful. Instead of having recourse to natural means, that would be too expensive, they seek some incantation of efficacy sufficient to make the earth temporarily swallow up the river. For this reason they study ardently the art of magic, a taste for which they have inherited from their ancestors, who have left traces of their proficiency in their Berbis and other edifices. The history of the magicians of Pharaoh is a proof of the application of the ancient Egyptians to this art.

"There is current in the Maghreb a copy of verses, there attributed to the Wise Men of the

East. It contains an account of the magical processes by which the absorption of water is brought about.

"'Thou who desirest to learn the secret of causing water to be absorbed, listen to the words of truth, which a well-instructed man utters.

"'Cast aside all lying receipts and deceptive doctrines, with which others have filled their books, and lend an ear to my discourse, and to the counsels which I give, if haply thou art of the number of those that follow not falsehood.

"'When thou wouldest cause to be absorbed the waters of a well which inspire affright to the imagination, troubled and uncertain on the means of execution, make use of the following talisman:

"'Draw the figure of a man whose hands hold the well-rope. Upon his breast trace the form of the letter *ha*. So, ——. Trace it as many times as it is lawful to divorce [three times], and no more: let him stand over the forms of the letter *ta*, without quite touching them, mimicking the step of a prudent and cautious man. Surround the whole with a line: a square is better than a circle.

"'Sacrifice a bird over this talisman, and rub it with the blood of the victim; and then make fumigation of sandaraca, of incense, of stactea and costus.

"'Then cover it with a covering of silk, red, yellow, or blue, without any trace of green, and without stains.

"'Tie it with two strings of woollen thread, white or red, of a pure red.

"'All this must be done when the sign of the Lion rises above the horizon, as it has been well explained, at the time when the moon gives no light. The moon must be joined to the fortune of Mercury, on a Saturday, at the hour when you perform this operation.'"

"I believe," continues Ibn Khaldoun, "that this copy of verses is a gratuitous invention of the impostors. They have many extraordinary practices and strange technical terms, which they employ in the exercise of their art. Other men push their deceptions further. They take lodgings in houses or palaces which are reported to be built over hidden treasures, and having dug deep, place there signs conformable to those which are in the books supposed to guide them. Their dupes, who are always required to make advances of money, are warmed by these corroborations of testimony and by the strange jargon of the magicians, and easily suffer themselves to be cheated of large sums.

"But all these doings are founded on no positive knowledge, and on no tradition. It is true that treasures have sometimes been found, but rarely and accidentally, and not in consequence of premeditated researches. There is no example, in ancient or modern times, of a general calamity which has induced men thus to thrust their riches into the earth under the care of talismans. The treasures spoken of under the name of 'Rakiz,' in the traditions, were buried by the Arabs in the time of Paganism, but are only turned up by chance."

After some sensible observations on the origin and distribution of wealth, which show him to be a good political economist, this writer proceeds: "The origin of treasure-seeking in Egypt is to be found in the fact, that that country was during ten thousand years subject to the Egyptians, who buried their dead with all their possessions in gold, in silver, in diamonds, and precious stones, according to the custom of ancient nations. When the empire of the Egyptians was destroyed, and the Persians became masters of the country, they opened the sepulchres to extract these riches, and, indeed, carried away immense sums from the interior of the pyramids, which were the tombs of kings, and other places. The Greeks, after the Persians, did likewise. In consequence, these ancient tombs have ever since been supposed to contain hidden treasures; and some are actually found occasionally. They consist of the riches which the ancient Egyptians buried with their dead—vases, coffins of gold and silver, and other objects. Accounts of these discoveries inspired the people with a taste for these researches. The trade of treasure-seeker has in consequence become so common, that when under the last reign the various branches of industry were taxed, a tax was also put on those who gained their living by seeking for hidden wealth. This burden fell upon imbeciles and fools, who spent their time and fortune in these vain researches. May God preserve us from such delusions!"

The preachings of Abd-el-Latif and Ibn Khaldoun seem to have had no effect whatever in checking the unreasonable thirst for easy-won gold. As I have said, treasure-seekers abound; though not among the fellâhs. These simple people, whilst profoundly believing in the existence of buried gold, profoundly believe also that it is impossible to get at it; and smile with contempt at the greedy citizens, who come like thieves to rake up their soil for wealth. Sometimes they fear that vengeance will be inflicted on their district for the impertinence of strangers; and therefore interfere, with violence or feigned stupidity, to throw obstacles in the way of all excavators. Antiquarians have suffered much inconvenience from this prejudice; and many learned delvers complain bitterly, without making due allowance for popular ignorance, or properly appreciating the philosophical moderation of those poor wretches, who will sit down, half-naked and half-fed, upon a stone supposed to cover the aperture of an inexhaustible thesaurus, and yet not pine with desire to possess it. It is true, they know that if they found a pot of gold it would not only be taken from them by the authorities, but would bring on a beating to force confession of another imaginary pot, the law that restricted the right of the Government to a fifth of the Rakiz being no longer respected.

THE END.

By the same Author,

TWO YEARS' RESIDENCE IN A LEVANTINE FAMILY.

1 vol. post 8vo. 9*s.*

FIVE VIEWS IN THE OASIS OF SIWAH,

ACCOMPANIED BY A MAP OF THE LIBYAN DESERT.

Large folio, sewed, 12*s.*

London:—Printed by G. BARCLAY, Castle St. Leicester Sq.

www.ingramcontent.com/pod-product-compliance
Lightning Source LLC
LaVergne TN
LVHW020241110826
845151LV00003B/995